THE CREATION SPIRIT

Dear Rich & Barbara,

May you always express the divinity you are!

Love and hugs,

Jim :)

9/06

THE CREATION SPIRIT

Expressing Your Divinity in Everyday Life

Book One: My Spiritual Awareness Series

Jim Young

iUniverse, Inc.
New York Lincoln Shanghai

THE CREATION SPIRIT
Expressing Your Divinity in Everyday Life

iUniverse books may be ordered through booksellers or by contacting:

iUniverse
2021 Pine Lake Road, Suite 100
Lincoln, NE 68512
www.iuniverse.com
1-800-Authors (1-800-288-4677)

ISBN-13: 978-0-595-39833-1 (pbk)
ISBN-13: 978-0-595-84237-7 (ebk)
ISBN-10: 0-595-39833-2 (pbk)
ISBN-10: 0-595-84237-2 (ebk)

Printed in the United States of America

JIM YOUNG'S WEBSITE

creationspirit.net. The website contains additional creations to come through Jim Young, including collector-quality photography. Speaking services and classes dealing with his writings are also made available.

"Great spirits have always encountered violent opposition from mediocre minds."

—*Albert Einstein*

Acknowledgments

There are many who deserve my heartfelt gratitude for their loving support of my creative manifestations and/or thoughtful feedback on this manuscript, not the least of which are: Deb Cawyer, Marsha Havens, Steve Sumner, Jerry Smith, Barbara Dicks, Joseph Horn, Myla Vance, Siegfried Halus, Jim and Margaia Forcier-Call, Manny and Janet Paraschos, Annie Woods, Ram and Seema Chugh, Bill and Lori Licata, Stewart and Marguerite Burgin, and, of course, other extended family members. A very special extra dose of thanks is due Alissa Marquis for her spiritual and religious discernment of the manuscript's contents; Carolynn Reid-Wallace, for her penetrating guidance which redirected this book to its current course; Margy Marshall, for her faith in me and her admonition to simplify; Christina Cross and Genevieve Paulson, for their clear and precise metaphysical guidance; David Spillers, for his wisdom, extraordinary talent, faithfulness and thoughtful guidance in bringing this piece and its companions into this format; and Dr. Pamela Finnegan, a brilliant novelist in her own right, whose extraordinary editorial skills and poetic sensibility made for a much improved text.

With heartfelt thanks for all they mean to me, and for the giftedness they are to the Universe of Life, I offer this gift to my sons, daughters and spouses, and their children: Alison and Stephen Henn, and Nicholas, Jackson and Katharine; Dana Lynn Young and Jonathan McAnnis, and Lyndsay, Matthew, Kyle and Katie; Kevin Young; Mark Young; and Todd Young. Likewise, this book is offered in loving testimony to my brother, Bill Young, and sister, Virginia Greene. May each of you receive from this offering an unbridled gift of love heretofore unexpressed. This comes, too, as a belated gift of thanks to my late, ex-wife, Jackie, and my ex-wife, Helen Jane, for all they have provided to enrich my heart and soul.

By setting this book free I also acknowledge my gratitude to Edie, Rachel and Brendan. Reaching such depths for and with them helped provide the spiritual spaciousness that allowed the richness of Innocence from which this book has come.

I speak to what can only be described as absolute awe and wonder over the nature of inner guidance received in letting these words come through me. Because of the multidimensional impact on my inner knowing, I have a strong sense that with the delivery of this gift of seeming eternal wisdom will come an ancestral clearing and healing of enormous proportions, particularly in the paternal lineage. Therefore, I express herein my commitment to ennoble the rich collective wisdom of that lineage, from my father, Harry P. Young (Aristides Yannoudis), back through his father, Pantazis, and on through the other patriarchs before them. I am grateful beyond description for their guiding Light.

A profound debt of gratitude is due Sufi Master Sherif Baba, who initiated me into Sufism with the name Ihsan, which he translated to mean one who sees Allah in all as his gift to them, formed by wisdom gained from life experience. For helping me to see myself from a more spiritual perspective, I am forever grateful.

And the last shall be first. I acknowledge and celebrate the freedom to create and its power to transform. I express my profound gratitude to the God that creates continually through me and all other beings. May we all "Be at home" to the Grand Creator within, living and lovingly expressing from that place and that alone.

Jim Young

CHAPTER 1

Emptying the Old Wine

I'd like to tell you a story about a widely renowned metaphysician in nowadays terms. It's early in the 21st century, and Christo Sahbays, a local healer, shaman, and metaphysician and his immediate followers of men, women, and children are beginning to be known around northwest Arkansas, located in the midst of the Bible Belt. Christo is asked to speak to a small gathering in Fayetteville, Arkansas, anticipating a hundred participants or so. Because of his rapidly growing, rather controversial reputation as a metaphysical healer, the demand for seats gets out of hand quickly, so much so that the decision is made by the organizers to rent a huge auditorium. Soon the demand again outstrips the size of the facility and they lease the university's arena that seats some 18,000 for basketball, overshadowing the sacred halls of academe nearby.

Some of Christo's closest followers begin to get concerned, the major issue being where they will get so much food donated for the concession stands, for they had never had to service so many people before. The women in this band of believers snicker at this, knowing that this would not be something Christo will be at all concerned about. When confronted by the men's concern, Christo shakes his head in utter disbelief and says to them: "You still don't get it, do you? These folks are not primarily interested in eating; they just want to be fed spiritually, even though that's not necessarily how they might speak about it. Can't you remember how you feel when we get into our discussions about loving creation? Do you really feel hungry for physical food when you are being nourished at a much deeper level?" They murmur and shake their heads in response, feeling ashamed of themselves for forgetting Christo's message yet again. "Now," continues Christo, "when the time comes, you just go out into the crowd and begin to share some of the stories I've told you, and mediate them for those who have yet to open their hearts to the world. You have far more than you need to feed these people what they want for real life, life in the spirit. As I have told you time and again, this is not an intellectual exercise. It's one of learning to understand symbolically, spiritually, the meaning of eternal life, not life simply in and of this material body," Christo finishes in a breath of exasperation.

When the day comes, the Followers, we'll call them, accompanied by other close spiritual companions who understand what Christo means by life, go out into the crowd that is amassing in the arena and begin to disseminate the food for thought as Christo has admonished them to do. This, in effect, is to whet the appetites of the participants for inspirational messages from Christo. As the starting time approaches, you can feel the wonder build and hear the growing hum of loving energy uplifting their spirits in anticipation of what they might find.

Finally the hour arrives for Christo to face the crowd. Gently he rises from his prayer stool beyond the curtains and gently parts them, heading deliberately toward the podium while scanning the assemblage. As he strides confidently across the stage, the crowd becomes remarkably hushed. Not a breath can be heard. Christo speaks "Namaste, ladies and gentlemen. I greatly appreciate your willingness to be with me at this moment in history. You are, after all, what makes history happen. Before we begin this journey together today, I want to take just a moment to do one thing I've always wanted to do in a setting like this." He pauses, and then broadcasts a wailing: "Wooooooo pig sooooooie!" The crowd lets out a communal gasp and then breaks into spontaneous hilarity. Christo has released the tension of anticipation he feels in the crowd and he can now begin with their attention unadorned by distraction. He senses that the hearts of all are nearly ready to receive the spiritual food to their fullest capacity, relatively unhampered by the tensions we all feel when impending intimacy strikes us.

He begins thus: "Before I begin in earnest, I want you to shut off all cell phones, computers, recorders, and put away all paper and writing instruments. They are forbidden today. Okay, you can groan if you wish, but part of this offering today comes from the overarching understanding and commitment that it is only through listening fully in the present moment that Truth can show itself. Just as in a conversation with a loved one, for example, or even with a guest in your home, it would be rude, as well as a detriment to the loving linkage established between you and them, to interrupt the flow of presence by answering a phone call or partly paying attention to a program playing quietly on the television in the background. Intended or not, such distractions do take away from the authenticity and the power of the loving connection.

"Applying the same sensibility here, this means removing as many distractions as possible from the context of our conversation today. When you do, just as when we go within with God, the heart connection is unmistakable. That is where I will be linking with each of you throughout the day. Let me say it another way: before we are finished today you will come to see that God is within each of us. That being so, is it all that hard to understand the necessity to stay connected with and respect the God in the one you are present with, instead of interrupting the connection in order to answer a call from someone else? 'Hah,' you say, 'but what of the God in the one calling?' Well, just know that the God in that one is patient indeed, even if she or he—or you—are not.

"Now, regarding the use of recording devices, as you will soon see, you don't need to record anything that happens here today, for all of it, and I do mean *all* of it, is already available within you. I will be serving only as a reminder of the Truth that resides in each of you." Christo senses that he has captured their attention, and he reinforces the capacity for doing so when he next opens his mouth.

"I want to begin our day with prayer. Although this may sound strange to you, I will say only that it is each of you who *is* the prayer that reaches the heart of God. Likewise, you are those who receive guidance directly *from* God. As you will soon see, this is what life is really about. I also want you to know that each of you here today has the same capacity for letting the expression of authentic love pass through you as I do. The only difference between you and me is that I *know* down deep within myself that this is true—and you cannot yet fully accept this about yourself. I also want each of you to know that God and I are One and, just like me, that you and God are One, and that it is God that speaks through each of us in our own unique way. Again, the only difference between you and me in this understanding is that down deep in my heart of hearts I *know* that this is True—and you do not yet accept this about yourself. This is the day when all this will be corrected. By the time we have finished our spiritual meal you will know without a doubt that because God in within each of us, this makes you identical to me, and to Jesus, for that matter. This establishes the Principle that God lovingly creates everything in Its image and likeness through each of us. Thus our self-perception is changed dramatically.

On Christo continues, through most of the day. During his presentations it feels like fine dining at an elegant French buffet: delectable and completely fulfilling, a meal worth savoring to the utmost. While he speaks, no one gets up to obtain other food or drink. No one exits to go to the restroom. Before long they are fully present to the Master, both the one at the podium and the one within each of them. Christo has hopes that all will come to the understanding within themselves that each of us wants and needs infilling, not from what is outside of us, but rather from the only location that makes infilling possible: within our very own hearts, seated at God's table. This is the food of spiritual understanding, which, when ingested and digested and assimilated, fully nourishes us and gives us life everlasting. The choice, then, becomes one of going either inside or outside for one's nourishment. One cannot serve both God and mammon.

Christo continues: "Today, together, we begin the process of reconstruction. What we will be doing together is tantamount to casting away old beliefs, the old wine, as said in Scripture. It will be replaced with the new, the long sweet draught of wine from the winepress of the sacred heart. However, in order to safeguard this new wine, our new understanding about what spiritual life is about, we must also replace the old wineskin, the mind, with the new, the heart, the container that will hold the new wine. The old wineskin is simply no longer appropriate. You need not be afraid of this process, for if you stick with me with all you are today, you will leave here with an entirely new perspective, a new consciousness with which to interpret and live your life anew. This new consciousness, a living, breathing consciousness of spirituality, purposefully brought to life from the heart, is that which helps fill the new wineskin. With practice, in no time at all you will find that all of life is an endless array of presents from God, as long as you stay present to life using your new frame of reference. The wisdom you will receive as continual gifts of grace is the new wine, from which you can drink draught after delicious draught.

"Right at the beginning I want to establish with you a clear understanding of what our purpose is today, and how that can lead to a much more wholesome life for all. Our purpose is essentially twofold: first, our purpose is to understand in the depths of our hearts that God and we are One, as spiritual beings created in the image and likeness of God. Second, our purpose is to understand that because this was also true of Jesus, that we are akin in our ability to heal others and ourselves as we collaborate in expressing life. These form the foundation for a spirituality of the Christ, the Loving spirit.

"St. Augustine told us that to know yourself is to know God. In the Gospel of John, 14, the Master Jesus said:

> 'If you know me you will know my Father also. From now on you do know him and have seen him…Whoever has seen me has seen the Father. How can you say, 'Show us the Father'? Do you not believe that I am in the Father and the Father is in me?…Believe me that I am in the Father and the Father is in me; but if you do not, then believe me because of the works themselves. Very truly, I tell you, the one who believes in me will also do the works that I do, and in fact, will do greater works than these…"

"Life is about getting to know thyself, and thus God, better than we now do. In the process we come to do the works Jesus told us we all can do; even greater than he did can we do. But this will not be possible until, and unless, we come to a more accurate—that is, True—understanding of what we are. And of what being created in the image and likeness of God means in the manifestation of our everyday lives. We're ready now to begin the first leg of this journey.

"What I will be saying to you early in the program will be thought by many to be blasphemous, even heretical. It will touch the nerve center of your belief system about life. The change in perspective will wipe away erroneous thought to such a degree that you will be spiritually transformed. But along the way it may well enrage you. This is the normal reaction to an inner demand for change of this magnitude. Be assured that if you do become enraged, it is more than likely because of the enormous degree of fear you are connecting with. Be also assured that the greater the fear the more important it is that you face it, so you can eventually come to a point where you pass through the illusion of fear to Truth on its other side.

"For the time being, what I ask of you is simply to give me an opportunity to be a bridge for you, a bridge that will take you from the world of thought you have been using up to this time in your life to a new thought form, to some new perspectives that will change your life in ways you cannot even imagine. All I will be doing is helping you see what you really are, instead of who you have allowed yourself to think you are. For the most part it will take only a spirit of surrender, a willingness to consider another perspective about what life is and how you fit into it. Then you can be a bridge for others when you leave here. God lends us to each other in this way.

"It is also important for me to mention that you will hear me reinforce certain aspects of things in ways that will appeal to some of you one time, and to others the next. Some time ago I was reminded of this sharing style by something that came to me in a very special prayer method I have used over the years:

I do not really give you new commands.
I have so few to give.
Only I tell them in different ways
so as you teach others
you can reach people with differing needs
who need to hear them
in ways unique to their resonance within.

"Whenever I have had the opportunity to teach, I am quickly reminded that as learners we are challenged to go beyond surface meaning when we are confronted by information and concepts presented in a multilayered approach. In this way, meaning can be fed not only by intellect, but by feelings felt, the spirit that is moved, insights that arrive, inspiration that turns ignorance into enlightenment, and the recollections we reunite with along the way. Sometimes this can happen within a single concept or a piece of writing, as with a poem that touches our mind and soul at the same time, making us wonder about its real meaning for us. Listen to this, for example:

Life
come, sit with me
let yourself simply be
plunge if you will, to the depths of your grief
loosen the slipknot on your weary body and ravaged soul
freeing your burdens
your anger, your pain
whatever it is that discomforts you
whatever it is you feel

come, sit with me
open to the joy that is you
letting laughter's release unfold your Truth.
allow yourself to bask in my love for you
healing your mind, your body, and your soul.

bathe in the Light of transformation
knowing that all you have to be is you
that I'm always here for you

come, sit with me
travel with me through the universe
be open in your tranquility
mindless in your solitude
resting your thoughts and feelings here beside me
fully present in this art of relationship
and you will come to know
yet again
that we are One

come, sit with me
no matter what the condition or circumstance
no matter what our past.
it is safe now
in Eternal Friendship the fullness of presence
is all that matters.
all we must do
is to be what we both are
and these intimate moments
become our Truth
authentic love our bond.

"Is this a poem about a relationship between two mortal beings, between lovers perhaps? Or is it about God beckoning someone to the power of relationship that can heal? Or does it touch you on some other level? In what follows today, I take the approach that we all need to be challenged and touched on varying levels, depending on our need at a particular moment. Therefore, a reframing of Biblical parables and Scripture, using personal references, penetrating questions, and pragmatic applications that have proven themselves over time complements information presented. So, if you hear something that sounds familiar coming at you from time to time, but with a slightly different twist, sometimes not, it is only to recognize the need to etch that particular understanding on the lining of your hearts through reinforcement.

"Perhaps it would be a good idea to give a simple, perhaps familiar, example of what I mean by changing one's perspective as a way of discerning meaning in life. Suppose that you find yourself in what you consider an intrusive or abusive relationship, let us say, with your boss. From how you see it, you say to your spouse one day, 'I'm sick and tired of what my boss is doing to me!' You could maintain this role of victim in which you have placed yourself—or, you could reframe your view to see that he isn't doing anything *to* you at all. He's simply doing it *for* himself, in this case to give himself what he thinks he needs out of life: control, power, attention, perhaps all three. You could just be the vehicle he's using to provide that for himself. You also could take the view that you are there to help him eventually see that very thing. In that case you could see yourself as a service to him. A more profound use of the case would be to see it as a metaphor in which what is happening is a clear indication of what you are disowning in yourself: that you are being abusive toward yourself in some important way and you have drawn this incident to yourself as an image on the screen of life that is dramatic enough to allow you to see yourself mirrored in your boss' behavior toward you.

"Taking this incident into your heart, you discern that if you don't stop your boss' behavior toward you, you are allowing the abuse, thus abusing yourself. It all boils down to an issue of self-respect, rather than the issue of your boss' abuse. So you have a discussion with your boss, lovingly pointing out to him what his behavior towards others is doing to himself, for whatever we send out comes back to us in manifold ways. You then point out that no matter what his choice, you will no longer tolerate this kind of behavior. Or, you could simply go on in the understanding that what he is doing is for himself and not to you, thus not taking umbrage at it and respecting the understanding that if you did, you would be taking yourself way too seriously. Be assured that if your boss sees that his bullying isn't bothering you at all, it will stop, period.

"Which one is the correct approach for you? No one else can answer that question. Only you can know for sure. The best someone else can do is help you reframe the issue so you can gain a healthy perspective on it as your loving foundation for moving forward. I guarantee that if you go within and are open to an answer that you are in no way trying to control, the right answer will come to you with indelible clarity. The more the answer surprises you, the more true it is for you, especially if it appears in a way that brings humor to what has seemed a tragic situation. That way you get both the Truth you need and the breaking of the tension around the issue. This understanding takes you to the matter lovingly, and you then can seek him out, lovingly offering yourself as a source of this wisdom. This is not arrogance, but rather compassion expressed for both you and your boss. The metaphorical exploration within gives birth to the proper rational response without. A changed perspective on how we think about things, about the spiritual meaning, works wonders. I suggest to you that this is exactly the kind of process Jesus used in helping others to heal themselves. Too simple? Too ordinary? We'll soon see."

Christo senses that people are beginning to see that there might be another way to think about life, because they're getting a little antsy. He continues, each word spoken from the bottom of his heart, each syllable authentic in its origin: "Let's throw a little more of the old wine out, so we can eventually create a much larger space for the new. I want to emphasize from the beginning that you will not find much of anything you come to understand today somewhere in books. Tradition is best passed down from generation to generation by way of clear and powerful storytelling: by word of mouth, so unique meaning can come forth in each recipient's heart, accompanied by the acceptance that is based on resonance within that sacred space. This is the spiritual tradition. For those of you who are Christian, Jesus taught not a religious dogma, but rather within a spiritual tradition. For those unfamiliar with this difference, the truth of the matter is hardly recognizable in the Bible—but I am getting ahead of myself here."

Christo tests the waters of change early, in order to see how much resistance he could expect by using this approach with those in attendance. From the somewhat jagged energy patterns he feels, he senses that the resistance for some could be considerable. After all, this is the Bible Belt. He knows, however, that as long as he simply gets out of the way and lets God speak through him that all would be just dandy by the end of the day.

"Unfortunately," he continues, "our world is losing its masters of meaning, primarily because there are other mediums now that have largely taken their place. These are but poor counterfeits of the original. Foremost among them came with the discovery of the Guttenberg Press, which allowed for books to be printed en masse. When we began to lose the truth of the face-to-face storyteller to the face of the printed word, the meaning of the message also began to shift, at least for the less spiritually sophisticated. When the real meanings in life were nearly eliminated by the depletion of storytellers, we lost the traveling schools, the masters if you will, that taught us meaning through story. Before, the listener could hear the message of the story within his or her heart, but when the written word began to take over and was taken more literally there was no inflection and intonation to hear, no communicative energy to feel, no heart to heart meaning with which to resonate—or at least not as deeply. So understanding has been kept largely on the surface.

"The more and more people learned to place their trust in the written word, the more and more they have taken it literally, and teachers and organizers of various religions began to indoctrinate their followers in their own interpretation of the word. This made it relatively easy for one to be a follower, for all one had to do is let someone else think for her or him, and interpret meaning for them, instead of allowing them to hear in the depths of one's own heart her or his very own authoritative meaning. Is this not idolatry defined? This is no different than listening to this message from me today. Each of you is taking meaning from it that comes exactly as you need it. Because you have been indoctrinated to live by the written word, and to find literal meaning in it, if I provided you with the written text of what I am saying today, at least some of you would take it as gospel and therefore in all likelihood miss much of its inner meaning for you. Once again you would more than likely test your intellect and try to figure it out, discuss and even argue about its meaning among yourselves. You'd try to make law out of it and begin to force it down peoples' throats as *the* truth, as the only way to interpret the words. This sounds exactly like what the Pharisees would have done: live by the written law rather than the spiritual law of God; living by what it means in the material world instead of the world of loving Spirit. The fact of the matter is that the *only* place you can get the Truth that works for you is by listening for the still small voice within yourselves and obeying it without fail. You'll never find it somewhere 'out there.' 'Be still and know I am here,' sayeth the Lord.'

"It has been said that Satan was born the minute collective consciousness reached the point of believing that being good would get us closer to God. The real Truth of the matter is that we are as close to God as we are ever going to get, whether we are good or bad, living or so-called dead. God is within each of us, is within all, so how much closer can God be than that? In a word, God's closeness doesn't depend on our behavior at all: God is within, period. It is only we who push God away by separating ourselves from the sacred by the ways we think and look at life. Look within: this is the only requirement there is for finding God. God is within—always has been, always will be. Anything to the contrary is but an illusion, in error, Satan by another name. It's all about how we focus our consciousness: within or without. We'll learn more about this later.

"I know that this, too, will rankle some of you because you have been told that the Bible is the *only* source of God's inspired truth. The Truth is that inspiration is received by everyone at one time or another, just differently by each of us; by some more clearly than by others, depending on how much of the literal meaning about life we hang on to as our source of knowledge. Yes, and depending on how much we are burdened by the emotional baggage we carry around in our situational knapsack that clouds our ability to receive the Truth from within. For the reasons I just mentioned, when the Bible began to be offered in written form the means of communicating the essence of the stories had already begun to disintegrate. Since then the written word has been translated into other languages by various scholars who themselves were raised for the most part on their own language and its intellectual impact. It is fully understandable, then, that one set of words or ideas cannot be safely translated into another language or from a perspective that cannot be conveyed accurately in another tongue. Just think of the game 'Password' and I think you'll agree.

"Thus it was that varying interpretations were made available for others to take as their own. So once again the 'hidden' meaning, the mystery, was lost. On and on it goes. This is not to say that the information and stories captured in the Bible and the Koran and the Torah, for example, are not helpful. They certainly are helpful, but they are not *THE* Truth that guides each of us on our uniquely individual journeys while traveling alongside others. We must be careful to such holy writ in the way Jesus would have intended them, and that is rarely in the form of intellectual literalism alone, but rather by going within to hear the Truth of the word from our own inner Authority.

"To put another slant on it, God doesn't like us to rely on the written word, for it is the word that comes from within that is the Truth for each of us. If the written word commands too much attention, it forms the patterns of belief that people live by, such as those taken literally from the Bible or whatever foundation pieces support the various religions of the world. Thus a rather rigid set of limitations becomes the lenses through which one sees and demonstrates life to the outside world. They become major distractions from our ability to see the light, become truly enlightened, within ourselves. This eventuates in people being enslaved to the literal meaning of the word, and surely God does not intend you or anyone else to be a slave in any way—indeed, if God intends anything at all—except fulfillment of the creation spirit expressed.

"God means for us to be free, free from *all* outside interference. Yes, I said *all outside* interference. Then we can listen to the still small voice within that speaks Truth and only Truth as guidance for each of us uniquely. In the Bible we are admonished to listen to *this* voice, to find God within and listen to what God has in store for us. This is the meat, the nourishment that the earth has not for us. In contrast, when people begin to absorb the written word as their system of beliefs, it is these beliefs they become enslaved to, and it is very difficult for people to even discuss them. Once people commit to a set of beliefs, they often feel challenged to defend them from invasion. God forbid one should examine one's beliefs! Not because they cannot or even should not be examined, but because it simply doesn't matter. All too often the beliefs have come from some external source, and thus they cannot really be the real Truth for anyone.

"It is much simpler, and more the way the Spiritual approach operates, to form ideas that represent current understanding from within. We don't get too attached to ideas, and when we let them have space to grow, they can form marvelous testimony to our Truth within. This is akin to how God forms Truth through us, beginning with a divine idea and then expressing it out into the universe. Ideas are the seeds in the garden within, and they grow as we express them without. Beliefs, on the other hand, only seem to help people cope with life, instead of infusing juice into life itself. All that does matter is that instead of forming our lives around such external constructs, we instead go within to receive the daily bread from our inner Authority. The voice you hear is the counselor Jesus said would lead all from within when he left physical life. It is the voice of the Christ, the loving spirit, and the Soul that wants only the best—our highest good—for us. So now choose: do you want what you fantasize as best for you and to live those illusions, or what is surely the Truth from your inner being, so you can live a life filled with peace of mind and a joy-filled heart?

"Now, consider this: The real Bible, the real Koran, the real Torah are not pieces of sacred Scripture we find in books outside ourselves; not at all. Sacred Scripture is that which we have had scripted, or inscribed—etched, if you will—on the lining of our sacred hearts the moment we were formed. It is here, within, that we must go to seek the Truth, to find the Soul's way for us. It is within and only here where we find the guidance of the Holy Spirit, of the Loving Way, that carries us forward throughout eternity. It is within and only here where we find the Truth for each of us, expressed in similar ways, but yet uniquely different, in order to accommodate the unique gift to life each of us is. When we find ourselves seeking an authority for living outside ourselves, whether from the Bible, or from our minister or rabbi, or some other individual to whom we have given up our power, it is a sure sign that we are either not aware that all Truth is within, or we are too lazy or too afraid to seek and find it there. Either that, or we have just succumbed to the brainwashing that has us going to external authority instead of valuing God as our own inner Authority, for the source of Truth It is.

"Religious authorities know this all too well and use it well to their advantage, for to claim to have the only truth, or the necessity to do your thinking for you, is the way they gain power over you. This is the way they control what you think and do in large part. Think about this for just a moment. The way you live your life is controlled largely by your belief system, and depending on your religious foundation, you will react to life's offerings in ways that reflect that system of beliefs. On the other hand, when you are following only the guidance from God that comes from the present moment within, you are exercising real control over your life. By doing so you have restored the Power of Divine Scripture that was inscribed on your heart the moment you were conceived. So once again, it all comes down to choice: do you want to live by someone else's, everyone else's, authority over you, or by the strength and power of your own inner Authority? 'I have meat you know not of,' and it is the meat, the flesh, the Truth of the holy word inscribed on your fleshy heart of which Jesus spoke.

"In case you are one who needs Biblical Scripture to verify this, we might as well begin now to convert the way we see Scripture, to understand the Spirit of it instead of seeing it literally. II Corinthians 3:2-6, for example, affirms this approach:

> 'Ye are our epistle written in our hearts, known and read of all men: For as much as ye are manifestly declared to be the epistle of Christ ministered by us, written not with ink, but with the Spirit of the living God; And such trust have we through Christ to God-ward: Not that we are sufficient of ourselves to think any thing as of ourselves; but our sufficiency is of God; Who also hath made us able ministers of the new testament; not of the letter, but of the spirit.'

"And in Chapter 5:17: 'Therefore, if any man be in Christ; he is a new creature: old things are passed away; behold, all things are become new.'

"Obviously, these Scriptural references are not saying that someone is opening up our chest and engraving the Spirit of Love on the outside of our hearts.
Rather, it is indicating with abundant clarity that the heart is the place of our
Truth, that which we already know and are to live: in the Spirit of Love with all
who come in our path, under all circumstances. The Scriptural reference is also
declaring that all our goodness of thought comes through us from the God
within our hearts and that is to be our sufficiency. It is not that which we find
outside ourselves to satisfy our ego needs, the external authority most of us live
by when we are not aware or awake. Last, the reference indicates that the new
testament is witness to the Spirit of God's laws, the loving way of thinking
about life, and not the letter of them, the literal translation of them that we are
to honor. Again, we are brought to choice: to seek our guidance in the outer
world of material and impressions of others—or to let God speak within as our
sufficiency, and to trust the Truth in our hearts as that which is to guide us in
our daily existence."

Christo takes a deep breath and links his loving energy more powerfully
into that of the crowd. He senses that they are with him to a larger degree than
they might admit, so he decides to follow his inner guidance now rather than
later: "Let me show you some more of that toxic waste, the old wine that must
be discarded before there is room for the new. I suggest for your careful consideration that the life and teachings of Jesus are part of a larger mythology."

Christo feels a surge of anxious energy coming from much of the crowd, but
continues in the face of it: "As you well know, mythology is a set of stories, tra-
ditions or beliefs associated with a particular person, group or the history of an
event, arising naturally or deliberately fostered. Joseph Campbell defines myth
as 'a lie that tells the truth.' Although I can agree with the truth part, I'm not
one to call the life of Jesus a lie, quite the contrary. What I am ready to say,
however, is that the truth that myths tell is metaphorical and about spiritual
life, not literal and about physical life. So for now this definition fits the stories
of Jesus perfectly, for such stories and parables do indeed pass on information
about practices, rites and phenomena of our Spiritual nature, this being the
healing of perspective demonstrated by Jesus.

"Moreover, what I am posing here is that we, Christian or not, all have an
inner sense, a personal image, a perceptual story about Jesus of Nazareth that
brings us into the context of our religious beliefs, how we feel about a personal
God; even about how we relate to our earthly parents and guardians, those we
saw as gods larger than life at a very early age. If we take these stories about and
from Jesus as true facts, but interpret them in a spiritual, symbolic way rather

than only rationally and literally, we can perhaps come to some very different understandings than otherwise possible.

"In a real sense, that is, reality based on our own creation, expressing the likeness of the Grand Creator we are, we can come to see life and all it renders to us from quite a different theological foundation. At the very least, our personal theological foundation can govern how we feel about life and death, and whether we are more naturally sinners than lovers who must be saved from the former in order to arrive at a kind of haven some call Heaven. In other ways, our theological mythology governs how we think about our relationship with God, others, and even with ourselves. It helps us decide whether we are separate from all others and thus must simply learn how to get along with them; or if we cannot, that we will be forever separated from them, suffering from the inevitable pain that accrues to feelings of separation; or once we understand the commonality of our being in kind, substance and purpose, we merely need to honor and ennoble that oneness with all the dignity we can muster. One thing is for sure: one's personal theological mythology is a deliciously ever-evolving one, as long as we stay aware of, and open to, the voice that speaks within.

"What this amounts to is discerning what kind of lenses we wish to use in viewing life; what attitude we want to apply to all life sends our way; and how we relate to the universe at large and all within it. Whichever way we choose to see our life, to think about it, we are choosing our heaven or hell. Either way, that is exactly where we want to be, for life will indeed be framed and governed by whatever personal mythology we take on to guide us through life. It is the bed we choose to sleep in, and sleep in it we must, until and unless we decide to change the bedclothes. As Dr. Wayne Dyer is fond of saying, "when we change the way we see, the things we see will change." I'm hoping that by now you are beginning to see that new wine is created automatically as the old perspective is discarded. When a door is closed to a particular form, a window is opened to a new world-view.

"I also pose to you today that Jesus was the Master Metaphysician, one who dealt not with physical healing, but with healing the erroneous images of thought, misperceptions, that create our dis-ease with life. Metaphysics is beyond, above, or deeper, than simply pertaining to physical life. It may certainly be a body of thought that effects and affects physicality, as we shall see later today, but metaphysics is not about the physical itself. I suggest this frame of reference within the context of a personal mythology about Jesus of Nazareth because it appears to me that we have done a great injustice to the teachings of Jesus. By placing him and his works mainly in the physical realm it is as though he were some kind of magician of the physical world who had and exhibited some body of supernatural powers. What strikes me false about such an implied assertion is Jesus's own statement about his works, if I may paraphrase: These things you, too, will you do; even greater than these you will do. Jesus's proclamation or admonition does not say that we *might* do them, but that we *will* do them. This being the case, then how is it that we may come to do so? By all of us going to some special kind of school to learn the skills mastered by the one called Jesus of Nazareth? This seems highly unlikely.

"What makes much more sense out of all this is that the healings Jesus did were conveyed in his mythology as stories about shifting, reframing, or healing how we think about life, and how a dramatic shift in our perspective on life can indeed change what occurs there. When we can free ourselves from the outside and self-imposed limitations on how we see life, our entire being shifts to accommodate the inner peace we feel and demonstrates our newfound, joy-filled heart. Once we free ourselves from those beliefs, perspectives, and attitudes that have crippled us in some way—the old wine—we become healthier physically, mentally, spiritually, and emotionally. We become more vibrant, alive, animated, youthful and focused on lovingly creating in the likeness and image of God that we are. The result is that our body chemistry changes for the better as our attitude about life shifts to a more loving nature. We both literally and figuratively change our being by demonstrating renewed health on all levels.

"In a nutshell, this is the personal theological mythology that I now find permeating my life, and one I now share with you from a perspective that in the beginning might indeed seem heretical. It is a mythology that is based on my own inner sense that Jesus knew that if people would only reframe their thought processes through development of new insights and perspectives and related sets of ideas, that it would affect and effect their lives dramatically. Jesus was a Master Metaphysician in his application of this deeper knowing. Indeed, his parables speak to this metaphysical framework in one way or another. In order to come to this same conclusion, however, one must also learn to see Jesus' stories metaphorically, as symbolic representations that speak to our life in Spirit, which just happens to impact our physical being as well. If you stay with the unfolding explanation of this personal mythology of Jesus of Nazareth, Master Metaphysician, I think you will come to see the sacred wisdom of such an approach for your own life. It can then be applied rationally on the physical plane.

"Another real life example. Recently an acquaintance described to me a particular take on the Bible, saying that the Old Testament was law and the New Testament, grace. I could readily bring myself into alliance with the idea of grace, particularly if one means by grace that when we go within for one's Truth, grace allows this Truth to be revealed before our very eyes, to see it in its spiritual meaning. However, I have great difficulty seeing the Old Testament as law, unless one means by law the law of the material world instead of an all-inclusive law that covers spiritual life. My personal bias is that spiritual law governs all, and physical law lies within and serves that spiritual law. But that is a conversation for another time and place. Instead, I want to cite just one source in the Old Testament that is used frequently to fortify the notion of law that informs our separateness—although I doubt that the users would think of it that way—and then treat it metaphorically. It seems to me that if Scripture is to be taken as law then it ought not be that which either encourages or perpetuates images of separation. Such propositions fast become the tactic of divide and conquer, instead of the amalgam of Oneness stimulated by healthy collaboration. The source I wish to present to you for enlightenment is the book of Leviticus.

"In Leviticus declarations are made about many and varied aspects of life in those days: rules for priests and individuals; rules about sinning and purification; about the clean and unclean; about what can and cannot be eaten; about leprosy and boils and burns; rules about conjugal relationships; and rules condoning slavery. It is sure that these were established in an era that, for the writer of this passage at least, had significance to the kind of life one was to live at that time in history. By careful inspection, however, many of these rules would be classified as no longer applicable, especially knowing what we do today about, for example, simple medical care. Yet there are those who would pick one of the rules out of obscurity and use it to justify some bias on their part, some denied or disowned potential in their own life, even if only metaphorically.

"For example, it is declared an offense against a family when a man 'lies with a man in the same way as with a woman: they have done a hateful thing together; they must die, their blood shall be on their own heads.' This single sentence, a rule developed centuries ago, is used by the self-righteous today to condemn homosexuals. Such people are sometimes quick to say that they still love the sinner, but hate the sin. Hating the sin is one thing, but to deny the sinner the same civil rights that others have is a highly unjust response to hating the sin. One is not denied inalienable rights simply for expressing oneself in a way that is unique to her or his sense of sexuality. Justice is determined between each person and God. Now, think about this together with me. Is it just for one to pull a single entry out of a book of the Bible in order to rationalize one's position on a certain topic like homosexuality? Either one follows or applies them all, or none at all. Otherwise it is hypocrisy at its worst. The rules, the way we think about life, are the rules, and as long as you claim one of them to portray a certain point of view, then all the rules also have to be part of the package. To do otherwise is intellectually indefensible and morally unethical.

"This means that if one were to use Leviticus to justify belittling gays, then how are lesbians to be treated? Nothing is said about them in Leviticus. Or does one just justify hate by inappropriate generalization? What about giving credence to slavery of women? What about the shame a man must feel if he emits fluids naturally during sleep, as a nocturnal emission? Using such things to discredit others or certain acts is the same deadly tactic that has been used to wage so-called holy wars and reduce people of color to something less that the rest of humanity. Again, if you want to use one rule, you must use them all—or none at all. That much I can respect.

"Besides, if one were to translate the meaning of the cited passage in metaphorical terms, one could just as easily see it as saying that if one were to place oneself in the understanding, that is, to lie with, the rational (man) in the same way one would with the metaphorical (woman), then they would have done a hateful thing. That is, one would have placed rational thought over metaphorical or spiritual meaning, and would thus have killed the Truth of the matter. Adding the phrase that 'their blood shall be on their own heads' is akin to saying that they would have to sleep in the bed they had made for themselves. If one selected rational choice then one would have to live only rationally, while the one who chose spiritual Truth gained by going to God within would have to reap the harvest only therefrom. In actuality, it is the blessed that use the latter to gain Truth and the former to point the way in expressing the answer gained from that Truth.

"This may be somewhat confusing to some at this early stage of our time together. A main point of all this is that when one uses rules or laws literally to justify a hateful action against one who could only be classified as yet another of God's children, then it gives license to any and all who would exercise injustice in this way. In spiritual law this is not possible, for in spiritual law lovingkindness is the only justice levied, no matter what the act. Spiritual law is not applied selectively. It is applied uniformly to all, contrary to the manner in which character assassins apply the laws selectively in order to justify their own hateful attitude. An often-neglected issue here, however, is that if one is homophobic, it does not mean that gays are sick or ought to be demeaned or washed from society. It only means that in some way the homophobic has disowned some aspect of sexuality that troubles him or her. This is more than likely being expressed as an approach to life that is primarily either feminine or masculine, when in fact, as creatures of God we are whole, to be balanced in the characteristics attributed to both genders. If the homophobic is a male, for example, then it is more than likely that he has disowned the more feminine qualities such as tenderness, acceptance, sentimentality, and compassion. Once he owns such qualities, or at least acknowledges his capacity for expressing them, then the homophobic tendency will begin to disappear. At last, I ask this: Did Jesus say anything to us—anywhere, at any time—about homosexuality? A change in perspective does wonders through the healing force it is. The blind can now see, and the cure is fast approaching."

After pausing to let this perspective sink in a bit, Christo begins to unlock the meaning of one of the most predominant stories from the Bible: "Ladies and gentlemen, given this backdrop for this next section of my comments today, I want to lay additional groundwork for the enlightenment that is sure to reveal itself. I want to approach this with you by illuminating a symbolic meaning of the Adam and Eve story. In this compelling story, God symbolically gives Adam and Eve the same choice he gives us daily, as sure as a beautiful sunrise follows each magnificent sunset: to see our world either through the spectacles of literal, linear, rational thought, or by simply listening within with wonder and awe for the Truth that comes through the Holy Spirit. The latter comes from God's grace that really is our only sufficiency. By going outside ourselves for authority, we would be taking over God's job of communicating Truth from within each of us by seeking it in the realm of someone else's view of what meaning life should have for us. The main reason people are generally dissatisfied with life lived from outside themselves is because no matter what they think they have created in the world, it can't really be right for them, for it is merely a figment of someone else's imagination taken in, rather than the Truth that wants and informs and creates only the very best for us. This is Soul's job, and no one can properly take it away from Soul.

"You see, when you finally decide that you will get out of your own way, that is, stop trying to control every detail in your life, and simply let life unfold for you moment by moment as the gift of Love it is, you will be served all the gifts of the Universe that support your highest good. This is the grace that is our sufficiency in all matters, under all circumstances. This is the meat that the outside sources do not have to nourish us. To say it yet another way, God gave us the gift of choice to choose to follow the dictates of that which only *appears* to be what we want from outside ourselves, or to choose the Truth of our inner Authority, simply by getting out of our way and letting it inform us. In today's vocabulary, it means to trust your own intuition, your own insight, and your own inspiration. If you're going to get drunk, get drunk on these interior images and not the material images from the outside. By committing to life within you live grace as your sufficiency and are never failed. By exercising life without, you are forever chasing the goose that laid the golden egg and your unique purpose cannot ever be fulfilled.

"I think it also is important for us to understand that neither Jesus nor any-one else commissioned the writing of the book called the Bible, nor did Jesus request that a religion called Christianity be formed in his name. Of this we can be sure. This does not mean that these are not helpful to awaken one to the life of Soul, but they are not Truth, they can only point the way to Truth. The contents of the Bible are not from Jesus, they are only stories about life through the ages and about how some want to remember Jesus and what he said and did. The last point I will make about this now is that because the Bible consists of stories about portions of history, they must be read as stories. In reality each is part of a mythology about spiritual life. Within this constellation of myths, we all have formed our very own mythology about Jesus and the God that informs and directs our lives. What I'm talking about here is the potential for you to re-form your very own theological mythology, not from the stories found outside yourself, but rather from your relationship with the God within each of you. This is your inalienable right and that which feeds and nourishes you in the eternity of each moment.

"On a related note, have you ever wondered what guided the generations of earthlings that came before the "Holy Books" were written? What did they use to inform them of the proper means for conducting their lives? Throughout life, humankind has used its natural instincts and intuition and inspiration to guide them. These are the tools that have allowed for the cultivation and expression of Soul, to permit the Truth to grow and eventually show its head into the light of day. For anyone to imply that we should live by the written word that has been only a recent entry into the world seems somewhat limit-ing, to say the least—and arrogant, all in one. It washes away all the goodness and loving-kindness that surely must have enriched the world prior to that time. It also dismisses those cultures, mostly indigenous and far from the reaches of the materially oriented world, that routinely operate lovingly toward all. Some would call those from a bygone era or from the outreaches of the world 'ignorant.' I submit to you that in this case ignorance truly is bliss, for such people were and are more than likely guided by their own inner Authority without need of any outside authority to tell them what to do or how to behave. They exercise life's journey with no second-hand maps to guide them. Again, it is the printed word—mostly the misuse of it—that has placed severe limitations on our communal loving existence. It is these very limitations that create separation between and among us, and those very same limitations need to be eliminated if we are to reunite in Oneness, both within and without. It is only the arrogance of the literal approach that comes from without that kills, mutilates, annihilates, and assassinates, not the Truth that comes from within.

"We must also be careful here to distinguish between religion and spirituality. Religion is a highly structured, written doctrine formed as a set of beliefs about God. In large part, man—for man's purpose, mind you—has developed and organized religion. I will not judge that purpose, for one doesn't have to go far to see that religion can lead us to find a better life. On the other hand, like every other doctrine, its teachings can be used to separate us from God, to divide us one from the other, even to annihilate others from existence. Spirituality, however, is a process of coming to understand, of knowing deep within, the God that is within each of us, and getting out of the way so that God may speak and act through us. It is a way of thinking that ennobles this purpose and demonstration in our daily lives.

"Spirituality is our most natural state, a state of being like a fire hose through which can flow the sacred, healing waters of the Almighty. We can also think about it as us being midwives to the continual birth of Truth that renders grace on one and all. So while the stories in the Bible may be fairly accurate portrayals of what God wants understood through Jesus and others, their downfall is that they are most often taken literally when they should be heard within figuratively, symbolically, metaphorically, for their deeper meaning. It is only when they are ingested, digested and assimilated in our heart of hearts that their real meaning most naturally comes and is lived through each of us as healthy and holy perspective.

"These stories, much like our old beliefs, form the questions, and within each question resides its answer. When we go within, the answer shows its face in the form of enlightenment. We don't get to do God's work. And, by now, we surely don't want to take the ego's way: over-thinking the answers, analyzing them, 'psychologizing' everything, or as I have come to think of it, 'anal-izing' it all. We let the God within, the Christ spirit, the loving way that releases Truth for us without being a burden, speak to us, and our yoke is made light. As you let go and let God inform in this fashion, you come more and more to understand that your heart is a sacred instrument, much as the sacred heart of the one called Jesus. The more you are able to see this acceptance of your Inner Authority as your sacred nature, the more trust you will put in this process for living a purposeful life, instead of giving your life away to some outside authority. This is akin to Jesus casting out the devils of evil thought, as he did on his forty-day venture into the desert, and then advising others to do likewise. When placed in a perspective that presented doubt instead of confidence in Truth, in essence Jesus merely said, "No thank you!" to doubt. In Scripture it is presented as: 'Get behind me, Satan.' So go within as Jesus regularly admonished us to do, to your own inner Truth, without doubt, and heal thyself.

"Now, with that in mind, I suggest we take a short break. I sense that I may have shocked some of you and it makes sense that you have some time to let all this sink in before I mediate meaning for a few of the parables. Then I would like to share with you some of the characteristics attributed to God, the Loving, Creating One, so you can see for yourself how you truly are the reflection and image of God. We'll then proceed from that as part of the your new foundation upon which you can reconstruct your life. We'll reconvene in exactly thirty minutes."

The crowd is astir from Christo' messages. They have heard some of these declarations elsewhere before, but they had been summarily dismissed by various religious scholars and from the pulpit as being blasphemous or sacrilegious. Somehow, however, these declarations seem to take on new meaning when spoken by Christo. When he speaks about hidden meaning, people are now beginning to get the point that real meaning for themselves can only be found within and not from another source or authority outside themselves. Each of them must find Truth for her or himself within and this could be achieved only by refraining to seek it from outside, or by inquiring only intellectually about a particular belief. This is an idea foreign to most, and it is confusing to say the least; confusing primarily because they are finding themselves part way between an old perspective and the new. What they need to do is ask for clarity from the seat of the new perspective entirely so they can hasten their internal shift in perspective. Christo sees the confusion as an opportunity for rendering this clarity and he sits quietly in order to gather the next steps from within.

Christo's Followers scan the gathering and collectively begin to sense that many in the audience are becoming angry. They report this to Christo and he simply smiles, knowing intuitively that being challenged to part from long held beliefs is sure to stir up the forces of anger. In fact, if that didn't happen then Christo would know that the real Word wasn't getting through at all. The waters were now troubled and he knows exactly how to calm them: with more Truth, this time portrayed through the parables, the spiritual perspective that would surely enlighten most, if not all, of the participants. He knows without reservation that when they become more comfortable with looking at life's stories metaphorically, which, of course, means how they would also come to see their own life's stories—for what enlightenment metaphor could bring—then the fear-based anger would dissipate.

CHAPTER 2

Hidden Meaning

As Christo heads back to the podium, he can feel the tension that had built up around the issues he had raised. He begins with his hands folded neatly at his chest and says ever so genuinely, in tones as sweet as jasmine in the gentle evening air: "Namaste. I lovingly acknowledge God within each of you." He pauses for what seems like an eternity and says once again, hands meeting at his heart: "Namaste. I lovingly acknowledge God within each of you." Slowly, very deliberately, Christo scans the crowd, seemingly meeting each person eye-to-eye, heart to heart. Then, a third time, he says with tenderness and sensitivity rarely witnessed by many in this crowd: "Namaste. I fully and completely acknowledge God within each of you. The only difference between you and me is that I *know* this to be true, whereas you are just now beginning to understand this Truth within you. As you come to this understanding about your true nature, you also will begin to acknowledge this Truth about and in all. Indeed, this acknowledgment will be your gift to all."

In this moment of Truth, he places his left hand on his heart and extends out the palm of his right hand. Instantaneously one can feel the extraordinary loving energy coursing out into the crowd. The tension immediately begins to melt away, and he moves on in connection with every heart, even those who at first seemed reluctant to let him in.

"While resting in the presence of God during our break—and you could just as well say in the presents of God, spelled p r e s e n t s, for each moment *is* a present that is the sufficiency we receive when we quiet our minds enough to recognize a gift or the present for what it is—I came to understand that it might be helpful to provide you with a few more tools to use in mediating the hidden word into Truth for you. Let's take, for example, the five senses. We most always apply them only to the material world. If I told you that the material world, all of it, is made up only of the essence of God, the ideas of God manifested, God's brainchildren expressed, as it were, then you might properly discern that life is all about spirit, or is spiritual. You might even come to the realization that if God created all as and of Its Essence, then we, too, must be of that Essence. This being so, then we would have to learn to understand Spirit by reframing our ideas about the senses into a spiritual understanding. Let me say it clearly, so you don't spend your energy spinning intellectual imagery and tire yourselves out. Your senses are for reading the meaning of the spiritual world as the highest order of meaning. To be sure, you can see, hear, feel, touch and taste materially and these assist us in coping with life in this material realm. The deeper meaning of the senses, however, is that it is really the senses that provide you with spiritual knowing, a deeply felt resonance with the Truth in each of us.

"For example, if, after explaining the meaning of a particular parable, I ask you, 'Do you see what I mean now?' you would most probably say something like, 'Yes, now I see the meaning from a different perspective.' Now, did you see the meaning with your eyes? No, hardly. You saw the meaning, or came to clarity in your knowing realm, by resonating with the specific meaning for you. If I asked you, 'What did you hear when I told you that your senses were primarily for learning within?' how would you likely respond? You would probably respond with something like, 'I heard for the first time that there are other possibilities for using our senses.' Did you hear that with your ears? No, I don't think so. You heard it with your inner sense of Truth. And taste? What would you say if I asked, 'What kind of taste did that argument leave in your mouth?' More than likely you would respond with something like, 'Boy, that argument sure left me with a bitter taste in my mouth.' Did you actually taste the bitterness? Not really. But you knew the inner meaning of bitterness you got from that expression, that taste of life. How about the taste of honey in a relationship? Have you either participated in, or watched with intensity, a particular sporting event and smelled defeat? Now, did you smell defeat with your nose? Of course you didn't. You sensed defeat from an entirely different level of being. How about touch, must we touch something physically in order to obtain meaning from it? Think about it. Haven't you been touched by a particular gift of kindness, a gentle word expressed right when you needed it, a sensitive portrayal of compassion from an unexpected source? Of course, each of these things touches and stirs your Soul, and you are moved at the very deepest levels of being.

"I take this time to present this realm of knowing to you so you can more easily understand that it is literal meaning that provides information, a beginning awareness that may point in a certain direction, but that it is metaphorical understanding that penetrates on a much deeper level than otherwise possible. Is it not possible that this is the real meaning of life's offerings? Is it just possible that life can be understood as nothing but metaphors whose purpose is spiritual in intent? Let's take a stab at how stories, parables, might add fuel to this fire of the burning bush, that is, the growing enthusiasm for the fire of Truth that emanates and purifies from within.

"I'd like to begin in earnest by looking at a simple parable to show you how seeing life metaphorically can bring extraordinary enlightenment to the fore. This is the story about the supposed healing Jesus did at the pool in Bethesda. As the story goes, the man had been lying next to the pool for years, and when Jesus asked him if he wanted to be well again, the man responded by saying that he had no one to put him into the pool when the waters were disturbed. Jesus was reported as saying, 'Get up, and pick up your sleeping mat and walk around.' As the story goes, the man was cured at once, and he picked up his mat and started to walk around.

"Now what do you make of this? That Jesus simply told the man to get up because he had faith enough in Jesus to be cured of his affliction? Nah, that's not it at all. It is true that there are faith healings, and to the degree that you put your trust in some outside force to heal you, healing can be manifested. You see, however, if Jesus's healing ministry as a metaphysician didn't consist of magical cures of physical ailments at all, then something else had to be at play. What was the *hidden* meaning here? Was it physical or spiritual?"

Christo pauses and waits for an answer from the audience, then continues: "Well, was it physical or must it have been spiritual?"

This time a rather weak "spiritual" comes from the crowd.

"I can't quite hear you," he mocks, "what's that again?"

"SPIRITUAL" comes a more resounding response.

"What?" Christo teases, "I'm still having difficulty understanding you."

"**SPIRITUAL**" the answer rings out from the crowd, echoing throughout the arena.

"Yes, that's it. *SPIRITUAL* meaning is what we're after in these stories that illustrate the healing within that becomes the cure without. Let's see how this works in this parable. I think you will begin to see that when we change the idea of something, we actually change the understanding of that something at a much deeper level.

"Okay, here's one *spiritual* translation of that story. What Jesus would more than likely have told this man was simply this: 'You have a choice of how you want to live your life, either our of how you have come to think of yourself—basically out of some illusional fear, and without acknowledging your feelings—or by seeing yourself as that which you really are and living the Truth of that. Either way, this is the bed you have made, and you will have to sleep in it. As a matter of fact, that is exactly what you have done; you chose a bed of emotional avoidance. Rather than deal with your own emotions, you want to use others, through which you can live yours vicariously. You want them to carry you through your troubled emotions, the troubled waters as it were. This is a disservice to both you and them. The good news is that you can cast away that bed whenever you choose and create another, but you must know that whatever you choose is what you will have to live with.' The pool in this parable relates to the pool of emotions we carry within us. Many of us are afraid to acknowledge our feelings, let alone feel them to the depths, certainly in public at least.

"Many of us fear them because we falsely think our feelings *are* us, rather than just a sensitive energy within us that informs us how we're responding to life. Fear of emotions is like any other fear: it is a figment of our imagination, an illusion—simply an erroneous thought—and when you walk through the erroneous thought to the other side, Truth is there for you. These feelings emanate from and are carried in our solar plexus, right here just beneath our rib cage. This is called the feeling chakra by some, one of many spinning centers of energy that inform us about how life is flowing through us. It is not my purpose today to teach you about chakras, but I will tell you this. Take your fingers and locate a feeling of energy about three inches from the center on either side of the lower rib cage, like this," Christo directs them. "Now rub those places, but ever-so-lightly. As a matter of fact I suspect most of you out there have shut them off, or at least they are out of balance, so if you probe a bit in these two areas, you are likely to find that they're tender. This is a sign that they are indeed shut off, most likely by the constant emotional bombardment from the outside world. If you want to protect yourself from most of this, simply close your eyes and feel yourself open these donut shaped wheels of energy just slightly. When you do, you are sending out enough protective energy to head off most negative intrusions into your emotional body.

"More to the point, when we choose not to visit our disturbed emotions, purely and simply we are disowning our feelings. If we insist on disowning our feelings instead of just watching them go by and acknowledging their energy, thus treating their display only as energy demonstrated, then that suppression will build and build and build until it finds another way to exit the body. For some, that will be in a burst of anger spewed out onto some unsuspecting relationship. For others, it will be an ocean of tears spilling out on the world, when simple expression of sadness would normally be felt. For still others it is tension released as uncontrollable laughter in the midst of a serious setting. If this emotional energy cannot find a way to exit normally, to be released naturally, then it will begin to coagulate and disturb the cellular structure of the body in a way that is unhealthy to your being—just so it can get your attention—like with a sore back or a pain in the neck.

"So when Jesus told the man to pick up his bed and walk, all he really was saying is that the choice about whether you want to witness your feelings or not is yours to make. Either way, you made your bed as that choice, and this would be the set of consequences that are sure to follow. The man suddenly saw the point and chose to toss away the bed he had made out of denying his feelings, and he was emotionally well again. He could then walk around, go on with his life—repent, if you will—exercising the freedom that came by living in spiritual balance once again.

"Now I will tell you this: if you are one of those who has chosen to hide your feelings because you are afraid to feel them, you more than likely will be pushing someone else's emotional buttons and living their emotions vicariously. Just remember that when you do this you are manipulating another for a false benefit. That's not how the spiritual laws work. What you really are doing is destructive to the other person because it is a form of emotional abuse. It is tantamount to playing with another's life for selfish gain, and it is a dangerous game to play. The only way to win that game is not to play it at all. That's so because if you choose to play that game with another, you are being destructive to yourself in that you are delaying a normal process of identification that allows you to feel what your body is saying to you, so you can shift the thought process, the perspective, that will heal it. Spirit works within each of us to see that we are informed as to what is blocking our spiritual path. If we fail to acknowledge this intuitively or instinctively, then we will be afforded yet another way—a second-rate way, to be sure—to sense feelings. If one continues to disown the feelings in each instance offered for this purpose, the cost rises until and unless one comes to the realization of this gift called emotion.

In the final analysis, if one fails to acknowledge emotion, he or she is sure to find disease of some kind set in, for it is not natural to store pent-up emotions in our human container. They're to be released into the ethers so we can be enlightened and our burden made light, all in one.

"On an even deeper level, our emotions trigger something we even may not have witnessed before: an inner calling, the Soul tugging at our heart strings in order to awaken the Spirit, our deepest knowing, to bring us into harmony with our purpose in life. This inner feeling is simply called resonance, and it comes from nowhere but our inner Authority, God, exercised through Soul. We all know this deep feeling when something feels just right for us. We also know this feeling when it shows what is really wrong for us. It is of the utmost importance that we develop this capability to discern from our inner resonance, so that we can follow and obey the Truth of its momentary message to us. To dismiss this, the most important communication from within, is to run away from living what is the highest good for us. While not usually thought of as even remotely similar to emotions, resonance is parallel to them in their purpose and ability to inform. We must learn to witness, acknowledge, and read such promptings; for this is *the* Word we must follow. If we are too busy to even sit with our innermost movements of spirit, how do we expect to know if they are even here, let alone what their message bears? Without this most valuable guidance we fly through life by the seat of our pants, which can only lead us to feelings of emptiness, for we would have merely lived a lie, an illusion, when we could have lived Truth for us instead.

"More than likely, many of you sitting here before me today are at a loss to understand what I'm referring to. Our society does not generally support such expressions, especially from men. This is not something to worry about, though. The good news in this case is that after today there won't be a person here who will not be able to go deeper into understanding their emotional body. This will lead to a keener sensitivity of Soul's calling, the deepest stirring within the spiritual body.

"Clearing the emotional body often serves the spiritual body. If, for example, you have been jamming up your body with latent anger, choked remorse, or bottled grief, although they have an immense impact on your emotional and physical bodies they also block the spiritual body from its natural flow of juice, of Spirit. Your emotions will find a way to release if you just give them half a chance. But as I said earlier, they will speak through illness if you are too stiff-necked about this. You can release such matters by beginning to understand that the pace at which you are living keeps most from even knowing their feelings are speaking, so numbing is life in the fast lane these days. Our job is to be a speed bump. Spiritual law requires that we put on the brakes, so we can slow down enough for enlightenment to show its way to a place many levels deeper than just awareness. As we change our pace of living to one that is more tranquil, we hear more and more clearly, feel more and more deeply, taste life to be richer and richer, see life's meaning ever more clearly, and are touched by the inner Truth for us more regularly. Eventually we come to understand that these messages are from our inner Authority, the one to whom we really are married. Most of us just don't know it yet.

"But first there is the engagement process with our inner Authority which allows for deeper and deeper discernment in such matters, beyond a thousand kisses deep. Here, too, there is a tug of war between the outer and the inner, between the ego-driven need to dedicate our lives to the outside world with its tasteless, empty offerings, and the nutrition we get from the Truth that we must live by if the Soul's calling is to be fulfilled. Just like our emotions, if we suppress the inner promptings, they will begin to show up in the people and surroundings we bring to ourselves, including our emotional foundation. All such things are metaphors that inform us in a way that we can see in the outer world what our spiritual life is like. You can read what's happening 'out there' exactly as you would dreams: symbolically. That's an important topic for another day.

"This is the purpose of your being with me today, to find out how to unlock the secret of hidden meaning. You have answered an inner calling to be here, and you can learn how to find your inner Truth before your very eyes. Pay close attention and be ready to give up some of your old-world perspectives for the new, the old wine for the new. Discard your old container, the old wineskin, and the old wine with it, so this new way of life, the life of sacred spirits, can be safely contained, for it is much more powerful than the old. These inner callings are the spiritual nourishment—Scripturally, the meat that not available in the outer world—but rather the nourishment found in our Truth that Soul requires for eternal life. Feeling free to feel on all levels of being places us in sacred harmony with the power of the Universe, and our lives change dramatically for the better. Give yourselves permission to let this all sink in, meditate on its meaning for you, and be willing to commit your lives anew. As I look out at you, I can see the inner stirring already performing its task of providing spaciousness around the old so it can be set free as a first step on your road to a new level of being.

"Now, a quick confession. Over the past few days I began to feel rather exasperated, as some of my followers have continued to show the face of ignorance. They have been traveling with me for months now, but somehow still don't get some of the points I'm sending out to those wanting to be healed. I use the term ignorance not to embarrass them, nor to judge them, only to stress a difference between knowing and not yet being able to discern Truth. The ultimate goal is not to have me spell it out for them, but rather for them to discern Truth for themselves by going to God within. My main point, however, has nothing to do with them; it has to do with my feeling exasperated. Jesus showed exasperation, too, and intense anger, tender love, and extraordinary joy. We all feel emotion if we let ourselves do so. We each express emotion if we are healthy. The real truth of the matter is that we must learn to read emotions for what they are, as statements of our inner being, the inner stirrings of energy that tell us precisely how we are relating with our core balance, our inner voice of Authority.

"To cut to the chase, I had been feeling exasperated because I was taking myself too seriously. 'What,' you say, 'taking yourself too seriously? What does that have to do with anything?' Well, it has *everything to* do with anything. Permit me to explain. In a nutshell, if I'm taking myself too seriously, then I tend to think that someone outside me made me feel this or that way. 'You made me angry as hell!' we say. Anger *is* hell, actually. 'You made cry, made me laugh, made me sad,' we say. There we are again, making ourselves a victim, creating separation and accruing the feelings of pain that accompany separation. This can only be true when we are taking ourselves too seriously. No one can do anything to you or to me; can make us feel a certain way. All they're really doing is expressing their feelings because that's what they feel they need to do for themselves in that particular moment. It may not even be a conscious expression, but it is one to serve them, nonetheless. To think that they did it to us is arrogant, egocentric, or even narcissistic at the highest level of receptivity. Or it could be that our reaction, that all reaction, is based on fear: fear that we are being discounted, abandoned, disrespected, or simply misunderstood. On and on it goes. But fear is an erroneous thought, an illusion that serves nothing but uncomfortable feelings.

"On the other hand, we have drawn others to us to let us see whether we are reacting or responding to their behavior. If we react, it means that we're taking ourselves too seriously, taking what they did personally, when it's not that at all. If we thoughtfully respond, or just resonate with it, then we're simply drinking life in, watching the richness of it's meaning for us in the moment. If someone 'makes us cry,' it's because we've drawn them to us to show us that we need to cry, not in response to what that person did or said, but because we need to unleash some pent up sadness about an entirely different event or circumstance. All the rest of life is the same, as but a mirror for us to see where we need to release emotions from another level of being. No matter what the reason, it is a good thing, for it releases the tension around that particular point in our physical, emotional, and spiritual bodies so we can come back into balance.

"So, you see, we might well want to thank all those who have, in one way or another, perhaps even somewhat inadvertently—at least from their understanding of what happened—provoked us to feel what we have suppressed, instead of having dealt with it at its point of origin. What they have done on a subconscious level is to have heard our spirit beckoning theirs to our midst so they could, also in serving themselves, awaken us from our emotional and spiritual slumber, so we could deal with ourselves on a conscious level. This works so profoundly in close relationships, where the potential for great healing is immense.

"As I just said in relation to taking ourselves too seriously, the key to learning about ourselves and what needs to be healed within is whether we react or respond to another's behavior. If, for example, we get even slightly irritated, or a heightened emotional reaction springs up within us when our life partner, for example, manipulates us sexually or acts selfishly, the fact of our reaction tells us that we are being offered the opportunity to look into the mirror at ourselves. Then we can ask how we manipulate, perhaps not sexually, but manipulate nonetheless, even if it is how we manipulate ourselves to do or think things that are really not for our highest good. We also get to ask how we are being selfish, perhaps not in the same way as our partner, but selfish under certain circumstances. The point is that in each instance that we feel our feelings elevate or our reactive irritation display itself within; these are the gifts that enable us to heal ourselves from some form of a disowned self. Thank God, for if we only react and miss the gift for what it is, then the emotional and spiritual debris will begin to coagulate and create even greater dis-ease with life. There is much healing that comes from this perspective, from the enlightenment that comes to us when we get out of our own way. All this takes is to slow down enough to find the healing that comes from a new perspective. Jesus did that. I do that. You do that. God does that, all of it, through the Loving Christ, the Holy Spirit within each of us. In that, too, we are One.

"So, in this brief story we find that spiritual life is really little more than reframing how you think about—see—life: looking at what you have surrounded yourself with and how it is affecting and effecting you, and making another decision about its value to you. If you want to change how you see your life, do so—reframe it—and what you see will change automatically. In this way, you become the miracle, rather than wanting miracles to happen to you, rather than wanting someone else to cure or heal you. You can do it all in this simple manner.

"This is in contrast to those who say that such a perspective is one that blames the victim. What changing one's perspective does is help us to see that we are responsible for what comes to us. Blame is not the issue or concern. The issue is the need to be accountable for our thoughts that always arrive at predictable consequences. This is just another way of saying that how we unfold into the world is all a matter of consciousness. The more we allow ourselves to be conscious of how we are relating what we really are to the rest of the world, the more spiritually healthy we are. Here's to your health! May we all drink a long, sweet draught from the winepress of the sacred heart."

Christo finishes with a mock toast to the crowd. It is so palpable you can feel the collective understanding strike people deeper and deeper.

"What we come to see anew comes to us through grace. When we get out of the way of our intellectual, literal, rational way of looking at things, grace gives way to innocence, the innocence of pure Truth untainted by outside authority. Simple Truth is our sufficiency. Is it not sufficient to have the grace of Truth guiding us in all aspects of life? Is it not sufficient to have all the answers we need exactly when we need them? Is it not sufficient to be able to regularly act out our most loving nature? Is it not sufficient to be able to link spiritually with all others and things in this loving dance throughout our span on Mother Earth? What prosperity this is! Indeed, God's grace is our sufficiency in all matters.

"Grace is that moment when we see the light go off in our head. It is that renewed perspective we gain by taking the time to slow down and step away from the network of outside invasions. In the moments of spaciousness we give to grace there comes a time when we find a new way to see life, and we are freed from the tensions that have formally impacted it. Then we can move on with a peaceful mind and a joy-filled heart. Grace is also the moment when we find a new perspective within which we can change our view of a momentary feeling of separation from another into one of loving-kindness. It is this change of perspective, this inner knowing, and this new way of thinking about the circumstance that renders forgiveness unnecessary.

"We don't need to enslave others or ourselves to the need to forgive at all, for when we gain a perspective that places us in the other person's shoes, we come to a new understanding that frees us from our judgmental determination about that person or circumstance. Forgiveness is in forgetting the old perspective that separated us from the other, and we move on in a new space that holds each in the embrace of loving-kindness. Forgiveness has taken place not because one has given it to another, but rather because new understanding renders the peace of oneness once again, and the tension of misunderstanding releases, is forgiven. We simply apologize to the other for bringing a warped perspective to our part in the misunderstanding and leave it all behind us. Leaving it all behind us without guilt or shame is the forgetting that completes the cycle of healing between and among us. Let's see how this worked in the life and times of Jesus of Nazareth.

"I'd like to do that by looking at the parable of Bartimaeus in a way that is quite different from the one you're accustomed to. Watch this scene carefully, now—with your new eyes—hear it with your new ears—and feel it in your new heart. Allow yourselves to really get into it. Jesus is walking down the street on his morning stroll. He comes across two of his friends, Bartimaeus and Thomas. The conversation begins with Jesus greeting his friends, Bart and Tom:

'Good morning, Bart, Tom, how's the day going?'

Bart responds, 'What's happening with you, Jesus?'

'Oh, nothing, I'm just taking my morning stroll. It gives me a chance to clear the cobwebs from my head before starting the day. You two look like a pretty glum twosome to me.

What's going on?'

Tom speaks up: 'Well, Bart and me were just talking about how disappointed we are with our wives. Both of us have been shut off from, well, you know, and we don't know what to do about it.'

'Tell me more, fellas,' suggests Jesus.

'Well," says Bart, 'I asked my wife how come she's so tired all the time and she lays out a list as long as my arm as to why she is. She gets up early to feed the kids and get them off to school, then wakes me up and fixes my breakfast, hardly eating anything herself. Then she sets about cleaning the house, straightening up the kids' rooms and outside in the back yard from the party we had the day before. Then she goes out shopping for food and such. Sometimes she brings me a coffee and treat at work, sometimes not, not very dependable, really; she comes home and gets dinner ready, feeds us and then cleans up afterwards; helps the kids with their religious and school studies; waits for me to come home from work and feeds me once again; and then proceeds to tell me she's too tired to make love when I want to.'

'Yeah,' says Tom, 'and when we tell our wives that the law of the land says that's what they're supposed to do, obey us, it just infuriates them, and makes things all the worse.'

'Well, there ya' go,' responds Jesus, 'you've nailed the problem right on the head.'

'How so?' Tom and Bart query in unison.

'There you are, you two, wanting to live by the law of the land, the laws created by man for man's benefit. Your thinking about life is exactly like a Pharisee's. I've told you so many times before that it's not man-made laws that life's about, but rather the laws from the Spirit that demonstrate as purely as we can the divine law of loving. It's in the spirit, the idea of truly loving, that we come to be in harmony with others and within ourselves, not when we blindly obey some law outside us. The latter can only render control, but it cannot render loving results.'

'I've never heard it explained quite like that,' says Tom.

'Me neither,' follows Bart. 'Tell us more.'

'Well, it looks like you've already forgotten our earlier discussion about wives submitting to their husbands, obeying them, and husbands loving their wives like themselves, so I'll give it one more try. This is not a story about human life, literally about you and your wives, although there are many who use it that way to subjugate women under their control. It's a story or admonition about that to which each of us *really is* married: God, or the Godliness within each of us. Women are married to, or husband with, their own Truth within. It is the ultimate intimacy with their inner Authority, or Godliness, to which they are married. They must live according to that and only that. The same is true of men. They must go to God within and establish their weddedness with their inner Authority, God, and follow the Truth they hear within with all they're worth.

'It is then, and only then,' continues Jesus, 'when men can find within the spouse the one called God, the source of all true forms of loving. It is then, and only then, that they can understand that God is within all, including them, and in that understanding they can love themselves by loving and honoring the God within. And it is only then that men can come to understand that they govern their lives not by subjugating women for their use, but rather by using the feminine within, the loving way, as their power in the world. As they come to understand this, then they can love others, including their spouses, as the God within all. When spouses, both literally and figuratively, are operating within their most natural bonds with the God of Loving Creation, they begin to manifest that same Loving Creation through all they are and do.

'This is not something they must force to happen, or even just make happen. Rather, each returns to open the way for God to love through them, the most natural reflection of Loving Creation in their thoughts, actions and deeds. It is tantamount to returning to, or re-membering with, their most natural state: Loving Creation. When each demonstrates most naturally this way a true Loving bond can be celebrated in every way. Then each loves others, all others, as they love themSelves, that is, the True God within. In reality there is nothing *but* God, so there is no room for anything but the Loving Way, except for that which we create as an erroneous figment of our imagination, just as you've been doing.

'From where I sit this is exactly what you two have done. You have created out of your imagination a view of your wives that is untrue; that they are to be slaves to your every need. When you can bring yourselves to see that you and your wives are equal in the eyes of God, and in your ability to act out of True Intimacy, then you will have an entirely new perspective on the real value of life and relationship—and your spouses—all in One.'

'Wow," says Bart, 'what an eye opener that is! How can we apply that to this predicament?'

'In lots of ways,' responds Jesus. 'First, consider that every contact with another is an opportunity to respond lovingly—or not. We are either responding lovingly—or we are not. There is no part way, just like a woman cannot be partly pregnant; either she is or she isn't. Now in this case, you might start by looking in your heart to find how you and your wives are exactly alike—or at least how you can be exactly alike. Take work for instance. Forget the externally defined authority for a moment and apply the law of loving creation, the inner Authority I spoke about earlier. Ask yourselves: Whose work is this, really? When you come to the answer that it all is God's work, and that as children of God we collaborate in caring for and about it by letting God, that is, Love, speak through you, then you are well on your way to solving your problem. Now create a loving thought about what your spouses do for you and your family. Think lovingly toward your wives with every opportunity you have and life begins to provide a corresponding loving attitude and action toward them instead of a judgmental one.'

'Hmm,' ponders Bart, 'I suppose I could get up a little earlier and help her. That way I would not only be showing her that I want to be her partner instead of the recipient of her slavery to me, but I could also be setting an example for my children in a very different way.'

'Ya, know,' says Tom, 'it occurs to me that this would begin to show some appreciation and compassion to our wives, so they would know we really care about them and are grateful for all they do.'

'Now you're getting the hang of it!' Jesus exclaims. 'Where are these new ideas coming from and how do they make you feel?'

'Well, that just came out of my mouth. I didn't even have to think about it, and it feels great, too! A lot better than the ways I've been thinking all by myself,' says Bart. 'I think a light just went on in my head!'

'I think maybe I just got out of my own way,' joins Tom, 'and I feel like I'm beginning to have peace of mind about all this now.'

'Good,' responds Jesus. 'Think of what just might be the very next thing you can do to right this situation. If the sandal were on the other foot, what would you want from your wives?'

'I'd want an apology,' Bart blurts out, without even thinking about it, 'and some help.'

'Me, too,' Tom adds. 'I'd be mad as heck if she did this to me, and I wouldn't want to do another thing for her.'

'Well, now you're getting into empathy, putting yourselves in their places. That's a good, a very good, sign, fellas, almost as good as the compassion your wives are expressing towards you by bringing your attention to this matter.'

'Compassion? How does compassion fit in?' inquires Bart.

'I would admit that it would be compassion expressed in a somewhat different manner, but it would be compassion nevertheless,' responds Jesus. 'Let me explain. If someone is doing something untoward, in this case the two of you are that someone, and can't seem to stop themselves, then it is an act of compassion to both them and yourselves to stop that unloving behavior, that unkind attitude—to reverse it. Once reversed, you are creating out of the situation one of a more loving nature—your most naturally expressed nature, by the way. In this fashion, the display of compassion heals the wound and changes the way all parties feel about both themselves and the other. There's not much in this world of ours that makes one feel better about her or himself than to feel appreciated—and helped along the ways of life. Authentic collaboration in relationships does wonders for all concerned.'

'I'm beginning to see the truth of this, Jesus, I'm seeing it for the very first time in my life.'

'Me, too,' chimes Tom. 'This is the very first time I've heard love explained like this; compassion, too, and I've got a long line of apologizing to do.'

'You and me, both,' says Bart, eagerly. 'Martha, where are you? I want to have a conversation with you about something very important to both of us.'

'Mary, are you in there with Martha? I need to speak with you, right away. Drop what you're doing. I'll help you with it later.'

'Before you run away,' admonishes Jesus, 'let me give you a simple way to guide yourself when you are out of sorts with the way you are thinking about a particular problem or situation. Let me demonstrate it using this current situation.'

Tom and Bart are totally focused on Jesus' teaching by now.

'Bart, how would you express your previous attitude toward your wife's reaction to your demands?'

'Well, I'd say that I don't think it's right that she should separate herself from me."

'Is that true?'

'What do you mean is that true? Of course it is. It really bothers me when she does that.'

'Okay, now answer this with a simple yes or no: Can you absolutely know that is it true that it's not right for your wife to separate herself from you?'

'Hmmm. I just know it hurts.'

'Yes, we know that you hurt. But just answer the question with a yes or no. Can you absolutely know that it is not right for her to separate herself from you?'

'Well...no. I can't absolutely know that.'

'Good, now we're getting to some truth here. Now, how do you feel when you think the thought that it's not right?

'I feel terrible, horrified, abandoned, angry as hell...'

'I can see that. Now close your eyes and look at her *without* the thought that it's not right for her to separate herself from you. Take your time. Look at her in your mind's eye without that thought. What do you see?'

'I see that I love her just as she is, and my fears and other feelings have disappeared. Actually, it's quite wonderful seeing her like this.'

'So, can you see one good reason to drop the thought? Please don't try to drop the thought, thoughts come and go and we can't stop them. Just see if you can find one good reason to drop this thought that it's not right for her to separate herself from you.'

'Oh…yes. If I drop the thought my tensions about this leave completely, and I feel much different toward her. She is some kind of woman!'

'Great. Now, do you want the truth?'

'Yes, sure I want the truth.'

'Okay. Now this is called reality. After all, you wife has told you that she needs this space to meet her own needs. She simply is exhausted at the end of every day. Is that not true? And she is behaving exactly like that, like she simply cannot do one more thing at the end of the day. So if that's what she feels she needs, and she's doing exactly that, how can it not be right—for her? Now it may not be right in your mind, but it is right for her. You told her you wanted what was best for her, but did you really mean what you thought was best for her from her point of view, or what you wanted only to meet your needs? And do you willingly honor her boundaries? Now, Bart, or Tom for that matter, this is not to criticize you, only to point out the reality of the situation. This process is completely neutral and deals only with reality, not with our imagination or judgment. Is what I have said true or not?'

'Well…yes, it is true.'

'Yes, for me, too,' Tom agrees.

'Okay, then, Bart, can you find some stress-free reason to keep the thought?'

'Well, I'd like to…no, not really.'

'Good. Now let's do a turn-around about this belief that makes you unhappy. Try it. Start with declaring the opposite that you started with. Now you can come to hear the truth about all this.'

'Let's see, if I'm to say just the opposite, then I guess I'm supposed to say it's right for my wife to separate herself from me. Wait a minute, that makes sense to me now.'

'Of course it does. That's the reality of what she's doing, so it's right for her. Now let's turn it around again. Start with: It's not right…'

'…for me to separate myself from my wife. Yes, I see that. By continuing my thought about her, I'm really separating myself from her. But that's not what I wanted!'

'That's right, you don't, but that's the reality, the truth of it. Good. Now turn it around once again.'

'How? Hmmm, by continuing my thinking that it's not right for her to separate herself from me I am separating me from myself. Wow!'

'Wow is right. Guys, there are three kinds of business in this world. There's our own business, everyone else's business, and then God's business. The only business that is mine to take care of is mine. Every time I do someone else's business I'm leaving mine unattended. And then no one is home to take care of mine for me, so I feel separated, not only from the other whose business I'm trying to do, but in reality from myself and the God within me. This is the terrible feeling of separation that overcomes us and is that which we really are feeling when we are anywhere but taking care of our own business. Now, let's make one last turn around. Substitute the words "my thinking" for the issue and see where it takes you, Bart, and Tom, you too.'

'My thinking about my wife's right to have distance from me is what is causing my problem, making me feel lousy. My thinking about my wife's right to have distance from me is keeping me from her and myself—and God. Oh, my. I see it now. It's my thinking, not the someone else's act that is what causes such terrible feelings.'

'There, now you've got it completely. Practice this same line of personal inquiry with every thought you have about someone else or for something that is troubling for you and you'll see the same kind of enlightenment. You'll also see that the real truth of it will allow you to take responsibility for all your own thoughts and feelings. Everything we see out there is only an indication of how we're thinking about life. All we have to do to change what's out there is change how we're thinking about it. It's your life, and you are creating it with every thought you hold as true.'

'This is so simple. I'm going to have to practice this,' rejoins Tom, with Bart following close on his heels.

'Yes, it is a simple and profound means to clear the way for the your own Truth of the matter, instead of living in some fantasy world that can only keep you off-center and feeling uncomfortable with life. This is the real meaning of dis-ease. Now get on with your lives, fellas, and treat both your wives and yourselves from this new perspective.'

'You got it, Jesus. And thanks a million for helping us see the way. I feel like my relationship with my wife has just been healed.'

'Indeed it has,' Jesus says with a knowing smile on his face.

"So often we have eyes to see, but see not; ears with which to hear, but hear not. What I have just described is something each of us can do, both with ourselves as well as with another in distress. We can help others reframe their outlook about life; help bring a different perspective about life's offerings. My bet is that each of you already helps others in large measure, perhaps in a different way, but you do it, nonetheless. Now give yourself proper credit for doing so—and acknowledge that you are behaving as Jesus did throughout his life, as the Christ, the God within each of us. Of course, you can also take the time to revisit such matters within yourself. This is the ultimate goal: to be able to heal thyself by going within for help. There's an old expression that says that God helps those who help themselves. As so often is the case, as it is stated there is something missing in that adage. The entire package ought to be contained and exercised this way: God helps those who help themselves—by going within for help. And going within for a more loving thought, the Truth about life, is the Spiritual path we've been talking about. Are you getting the point yet?

"Let's see if you are. How many of you have helped someone in somewhat the same way as that described in my mediation of the parable about Bartimaeus? Raise you hand."

Nearly every hand shoots up in acknowledgment.

"Wow, there you have it!" exclaims Christo. "In so doing you have exhibited the same healing power as Jesus did in this story. All it takes is the power of attentive listening, a touch of empathy and sympathy, and a reframing of old perspectives into those that can heal the situation. Now let this revelation that you and Jesus have the same power to heal sink in, as a basis for more that is sure to follow."

Christo pauses and takes a deep breath. He senses that the crowd is benefiting not only from the spiritual messages he has been delivering, but that the growing collective loving energy also is having an enormous impact on the crowd. The healing aspect is running full tilt. He feels that the time is just right for the crowning blow, the last story he is to open up to the Truth for them. Taking a long, deep breath, Christo begins: "I want to finish this segment with one last story. It is the story that describes Jesus's death on the cross, for this explains his purpose for coming to us those many years ago. I ask once again that you take this into your hearts and refrain from intellectualizing it, from analyzing it against your current beliefs. I think you'll see what I mean rather quickly if you follow my admonition in this regard.

"The story about Jesus's death is extraordinarily dramatic when taken literally, and very painful for any who take it into their emotions. Let me describe the suggested scenario and reframe it into spiritual Truth, so that your minds can be cleansed from error, so you can take a very different perspective away with you, at least as a possibility for further discernment. Let's begin with the scene at what's called 'the Last Supper.' You will find it referenced in Luke: 22, 19-20. We are lead by some to believe that the Eucharist is actually Jesus' body and blood, and that to commune in this fashion is to unite us with him each time we do. Not to be disrespectful, but I recall such things being taught during catechism class while I was a youngster, and being repulsed by the thought of drinking blood and eating flesh. Perhaps that is why I didn't take those classes as seriously as one might. Surely, I thought, Jesus did not mean for the apostles, even for us as Christians, to replicate the life of cannibals. So, it appears to me that there must be some other meaning. You guessed it; it must be a spiritual meaning instead of literal.

"There are several meanings that are more appealing than what has been offered so far. The first relates to the loving-kindness that exudes from immersing oneself in breaking bread and drinking wine with fellow believers. One is filled to the brim with feelings of love and the gift of deep intimacy that ensues. Could Jesus not simply mean that we should emulate this last supper by bringing our families and/or friends together in a similar way in order to celebrate deep and abiding relationship? Can you just imagine how much more devoted family members and friends would be towards one another if this were a regular practice? And just think what could come of expanding such an idea to every meal we eat, with whomever we choose?

"There is a another meaning for Jesus's words that I also favor. Of course, the only meaning for you is the one that rings true, or resonates, in your heart of hearts. Well, we all know by now that bread is that which comes to us as the Word, the sacred transmission of Truth from each of us as we listen faithfully within. This is the bread of life. Is Jesus not reminding us here that we are to go within for our daily bread? In fact, is this admonition not contained in what is called The Lord's Prayer? And also contained in the wine? Is wine not the Loving Spirit we call the Christ that flows through us as God's divinely loving ways? Is Jesus not reminding us here that when we get out of our own way the Love of God flows from our sacred hearts to all we touch? You will have to discern all this for yourselves, but at least now you know that there are some options to dining on such a gruesome literal menu.

"To continue, I'm sure you will recall Jesus standing before Pontius Pilate, the judge, if you will. He stated certain accusations and asked Jesus to respond to them. In each case, except one, Jesus did not respond. 'Why didn't he defend himself?' you might ask. The answer is a very simple one. By answering the charges he would have given dignity to them when they didn't deserve dignity. Also, it could well have provided the opportunity to divide those who heard them into believers and nonbelievers, and there we have separation, not oneness in spirit. Jesus's life was about teaching us to live in the Oneness that eliminates separation and duality, so he would not go that way. He was single-minded about this.

"An additional point Jesus was making, and it is critical to understand this, is that unless the God within speaks through someone, what they are saying is nothing but a figment of their imagination, their ego—a made up story, a fantasy, and thus an illusion. The reality of this situation also speaks to the Truth that it is none of our business what anyone else thinks or says about us, pure and simple—*none* of our business—for if we are paying attention to such matters, then we will more than likely be taking ourselves too seriously, plus taking such things personally, when they are only a figment of someone else's creation constructed for themselves. This figment tells us something only about the person's attitude that made the comment. It says absolutely *nothing* about us. To say that it does is narcissistic. Any response at all reinforces such dysfunction. The only real business I have is that I know within myself what I am and, seated in the intimacy of my likeness of God, the image of loving and loving only, I know that my acts have been nothing but that, no matter what anyone else says. When I walk in my own Truth, the Truth of what I am and how I manifest that throughout my life, I need no defense. I only need to be steadfast in that knowing. When I do, I know that no accusation to the contrary can tear me down, nor will I allow it to do so. If I do allow someone to diminish me, then I am making him or her my outer authority. Rather, the way of self-respect and fullness of dignity would have me simply walk in my Truth and ignore the details, thus standing in the Truth of my own inner Authority. Besides, it's not my business to take responsibility for what anyone else thinks. Only they can and should do that.

"Now, when Jesus was placed before the people by Pilate, Pilate gave them the opportunity to choose between being judgmental or simply letting Jesus be what he was. Out of their own need to be judgmental, they did just that. Threatened by Jesus' stance, his ability to stand in his own inner integrity when most yet could not, they wanted him removed from the scene so they wouldn't have him as a reminder of their own ineptitude any longer. This is very much like those who would want you removed from their presence when you represent some threat to their emotional stability. Most simply want to continue on the safe, comfortable, familiar path they have traveled on throughout most of their lives. It is painful to think of another way, one in which they might have to give up old beliefs, old marriages to outworn or untruthful thinking, in order to be born again into a more healthy state. The anguish of not knowing how to get from where they are to a place that seems so foreign to them is simply too painful. Often, they end up pushing you away, in some cases violently, just so they won't have to face themselves and declare a new road upon which to travel. The eye of the needle is that small for them. This is an essential element of failed relationships.

"But that has nothing to do with you, *per se*. That is, it is nothing you did that caused it. There is nothing to take personally. In fact nothing is ever be taken personally, for each person's thoughts and actions are only what they manifest for their own purpose and have absolutely nothing to do with you. It is merely that another was reacting to what you are, and even though they saw and may have temporarily liked it, it simply became too uncomfortable within them to continue. As it is reported that Jesus said, simply shake the dust off your sandals and move on to those who want what you have and are. A main point here, once again, is that it's none of your business what anyone else thinks about you. Your only job is to be what you are, loving essence, and to let that shine in and through all you do. Period. In this way, just as the example Jesus was, you are always working to collaborate in erasing separation and inserting loving Oneness in its place.

"To continue with the story, there were those along the way who thought that Jesus needed assistance in carrying his cross, the loving way that he had chosen for himself. I'm sure Jesus would admit that even he had difficulty carrying this cross sometimes. People just didn't get what his purpose was, to clear the way for Oneness by eliminating the mindless causes for separation. Although he did permit one to assist him, he came to the quick realization that it was only he who could and should shoulder that responsibility. No one else could carry it for him—or us. Much like the man who made his bed of not allowing him to go into the emotional waters in order to heal himself, the loving way is the bed Jesus made for himself and he alone had to sleep in it, just as we will.

"The part of the story that had the centurions gambling for Jesus's clothes makes its own point. Some may well have wanted the souvenirs for whatever reason, while some others secretly may have connected with Jesus and wanted to carry forward the symbol of clothes as the loving nature he had worn throughout his life on earth. And although Jesus is most always depicted otherwise, he was hanged totally naked, a symbol of total humiliation according to the opposition. More important to this way of framing the story, however, he was standing naked before God, as each one of us must learn to do each moment of our lives. We don't need to cloak ourselves intellectually, emotionally or spiritually, and when we do we are gambling that we can cover ourselves up or fool someone. The only someone that really matters in spiritual life is God, and God sees only our unadorned heart and the clarity of our soul. Whether we think we are somehow disguising ourselves or not, our Truth, the way God sees us, is forever the same, disguises to the contrary. When we stand naked in our thoughts before God, we are surrendering to God's means of innocence, filling our minds with the divine, which, over time, will render our world the very same. Once we get the hang of thinking of the world we see as divine, it becomes automatic in us, as well as in our expressions about it.

"Those who don't yet act and believe in this way wear the cloaks of guilt, shame, fear, and error, garnered from erroneous thoughts about ourselves and those around us. The point here is that you can't really fool God; so don't try to fool yourself either, for each of you is made in the image and likeness of God. This means that you are not born in original sin, but rather that you are the essence of God, each expressed uniquely as you. When you finally let yourself acknowledge this and know it in the depths of your heart, you will begin to live it as your most natural self. There will be no other way. But if you dress yourself, your heart, your deepest thoughts, in one cloak or another, your life will be shaded by that view of yourself instead.

"It is time to shed all the cloaks, all of the roles in which you place yourself, and come to stand naked before the world as the child, God's idea of you, that you are. In this way, you finally clear from the heart all the debris that keeps you from seeing and demonstrating its only purpose: the utmost in loving intimacy, both with God and yourself. This powerful space forces out all forms of fear and sets you free to live intimately. This ultimate intimacy affords you the foundation from which you can then demonstrate intimacy on every level, with one and all, and with all that supports life on this planet. But until you reach this point you will be living a simple counterfeit of the real thing. Once again, the choice is yours. Is it separation or Oneness you want?

"Permit me now to clarify the symbolism of the cross. It is not one of agony related to Jesus's death. Nor is it to be associated with his dying for your sins. Quite simply, the vertical reference of the cross symbolizes the deep, passionate and abiding relationship we must each have with our God within. We go deep down, within, in order to hear the voice of our God. The horizontal plane represents the deeply compassionate relationship we must reach out with to our collaborators in loving creation: all other entities on the planet. The nailing of Jesus' feet to the cross emphasizes the truth that he is anchored to that intimate relationship with God, his inner Authority within. Each one of must also be anchored in that same reality instead of in the illusory thoughts we have about that which is without. Equally so, he was anchored to his compassionate relationship with all who came into his path, as his hands were nailed in this welcoming position on the cross he chose to carry, as his path of loving-kindness. Each of us must also be about extending our passionate love for God to all others compassionately. We can love another only as deeply as we love God and ourselves. So rather than get caught up in some manufactured reasoning about Jesus' death, simply remember that all of life is a symbol or metaphor that serves its spiritual meaning. It is always the case that life can be read for our spiritual benefit, even though it also may have some practical, rational meaning as well.

"Furthermore, when Jesus asked God for help, when he wondered if God had forsaken him, he was showing that even though each of us is to walk the path of loving-kindness, when we are in highly stressful situations our behavior often resorts to old, no longer useful patterns. Finally, Jesus relented and died to that old pattern, fully letting himself go to fulfilling his intended purpose on planet earth. Along the way, of course, he did ask that those who were considered criminals come to see themselves as merely those who had made mistakes. We all make mistakes from time to time, mostly when we apply some fearsome thought to a problem or issue at hand. We are so used to doing so that we act this way almost automatically. We don't even realize that we are using an erroneous process to try to manifest a truthful life of inner joy and a peaceful mind. All it takes is a forgiving of ourselves, a well as a forgetting of the past, in order to renew our thinking and the ways of manifesting life. Jesus's statement that the criminals and others didn't know what they were doing also describes the fact that they, like most people, act out of their relationship with the outer world rather than with the reality of the inner one. If everyone acted only out of his or her inner relationship with Loving, this would indeed be a very different world.

"And Jesus's so-called resurrection? Of course, it's about transformation; about a new life that emits in the darkest moment; it's about justice, mercy and compassion. Mostly, though, this part of the story is to disavow the idea of death. To be sure, the human form comes into existence and leaves that form at some time, but life itself goes on spiritually. Life is not about material form, but rather spiritual being, living the loving essence we are through all we are and do. As humans we are much like mosquitoes: they come into this life, they move on, and have nothing but a veritable feast in between. It is our natural essence to love, and we continue to love creations and love creating, no matter in what form, throughout eternity. This is our veritable feast. It always has been, is, and always will be that for us. Those who remain after we change form from human to spirit once again can maintain regular contact by dropping the limitation of thought that keeps it from happening. The contact may be made through the sleeping dream state or the awakening dream state, or through a medium that has exercised the capacity to communicate in case you cannot bring yourself to do so. Let go of your limitations, just as the Apostles in the story had to do, so you can traverse in Spirit within and between various states of being. It's as simple as that. But limitations against it must first be removed in order to make it possible.

"Jesus's purpose then, just in case you missed it, was to awaken us to the reality that this life is meant to show us that real life is nothing but spiritual and that whatever we see outside ourselves is but a wonderful mirror to show us the current reality of our inner life, how we are thinking about it. This is what makes our lives sacred: knowing even the mundane as sacred. Being aware of that, we can become expert at cleaning out those 'treasures' of erroneous beliefs that no longer serve us in the wake of enlightenment. As it central thesis, his purpose is found in the fact that God is omniscient, omnipotent, omni-present, and omni-active. Being so, there is nothing but the essence of God, and that includes us in its Oneness. There is only God. There is not God *and…*

"This finally brings us to the understanding that separation is indeed impossible, no matter what configuration of thought or belief we can muster. Once having come to that Truth for all of life, we understand that extending to all others our passion for loving God compassionately is our most natural way of life, for Loving *is* our nature. So when it is said that Jesus died for our sins, we must conclude that the symbolism indicates that we all must die *to* that which is our *only* sin: going without to some external authority when we know that the only real, that is, True, Authority is that which shows its face when we unite with God within. We must not forget that each of us has God within, so when someone else triggers resonance within ourselves by some comment that comes from his or her God within, it unites us in Oneness again. Once again, this is the ultimate in understanding that in the reality of spiritual life there is no separation, only Oneness. Each time we point to, or unite with, the outside world as some authority, we create separation and we obviate the path to Truth.

"The last thing I want to tell you about this is to indicate with absolute clarity that leading you to see these elements of the story of Jesus's death in a very different way is neither to indicate that Jesus did not actually die on the cross, nor that he never even existed at all. Quite the contrary. My purpose is merely to lead you to see that whatever is presented from the outside as an act that in fact can be true is primarily, if not solely and soulfully, for the purpose of understanding the profound nature of our spiritual life.

"I've gone on long enough about this story. Let its various elements settle into your hearts, refraining from the normal simple intellectual analysis we so often apply. Unfortunately, linear, rational thinking does not provide Truth. It only provides information that can head us in certain directions. Let simple awe and wonder determine their meaning for you, not only in reference to this story, but also for all of life. When you finally trust awe and wonder in place of your literal interpretation of life, you will come to Truth instead of the fabricated facsimile that can only be created out of one's own thoughts. When something comes into play on your screen of life, don't try to figure it out. Get out of your own way and settle into the awe of such imagery appearing before you, knowing that it is showing up to provide you with the gift of symbolism necessary for your spiritual welfare; to assist you in your daily life. When it shows up, merely say in your heart, 'I wonder what this is all about.' Then get out of your own way, your intellectual chase for the answer, and watch the real answer come to the fore. It will come very quickly if you simply trust for it to be there for you in the depths of your sacred heart.

"When we go outside of ourselves for answers we automatically establish a world of duality: them and me, better or worse; a world of separation and all the pain that separation engenders. We do this also when we place God outside ourselves, as some entity that holds all the sugar for nourishing us in life. It is the deep feeling of separation from God that pains us at the Soul level, that shows its way into our feelings of separation from all others, even from the environment that supports us so richly. It is duality personified. When, on the other hand, we continually acknowledge our oneness with God and seek our nourishment only from that inner source, we also soon come to realize our connectedness to the rest of the world. We will have come to see the God in all and thereby give all the dignity they deserve. In this single Truth about life, duality is thus rendered nonexistent in that moment, and loving abounds.

"If you are having feelings of separateness, of feeling disconnected from the rest of the world, I suggest to you that there are ways to shift this imagery so you can heal yourself. For example, Kahlil Gibran wrote, 'The spirit of Jesus of

Nazareth is the best and oldest wine…His heart was a winepress. You and I could approach with a cup and drink therefrom.' Should we choose, you and I could drink a long, sweet draught of his wine, his spirit, the way he thought about life, the epitome of loving, and partake in this relationship: Loving fully expressed, openly accepted, and completely embodied. The more passionately we give of ourselves to compassionate loving the greater the quality of fruit in our winepress, and the finer, more mature, full-bodied is the resulting wine, or Spirit, of relationship. The need for relationship is thus affirmed. It is the wine that connects us in the Oneness we are with God, and in one another, all as the normal outcome of Ultimate Intimacy.

"Do this visualization with me now if you will, and it will give you a way to be the miracle of healing itself. Close your eyes and see yourself with a wine barrel spigot coming out from your sacred heart. Place yourself in the understanding that your only purpose in life is to keep this spigot from which flows only the best wine, open, so that others may drink the purest form of loving spirit from your loving, sacred heart. Now, in your heart's eye, see all others on the planet with the same kind of spigot, and notice that they, too, understand that keeping the spigot open to nourish others is their only purpose in being. Find someone in that array of people with whom you are having some difficulty, or for whom you have some hard feelings. See yourself offering that person a long, sweet draught of your loving spirit. See them reach out with their cup, filling it to overflowing. Now reach out to his or her spigot and fill your cup with the same intent. Notice your feelings as you now visualize this. In all likelihood, you have just witnessed a breath of fresh air that sweeps away the pain you witnessed by being separated from that other—and you both are healed, restored to loving Oneness.

"Now open your eyes and look around you. More than likely you will see everyone else in this arena lit by the unfettered sharing of loving spirit. That is the unmistakable glow of enthusiasm for passionately loving ourselves and our brothers and sisters alike. You will notice, too, I am sure, that it has made no difference whether someone is black or white or yellow, male or female, straight or gay. The loving glow connects us all as One. You can do this exercise anytime you wish, each time with the same results. The real key to peace of mind and the fullness of a joyful heart, however, is to visualize yourself walking through life with your spigot open for all to drink from in unlimited fashion. It is your sole, and Soul, job to lavish all with loving spirits. This key will unlock the door that opens us to Oneness when we recognize that others also have this same obligation to the loving way, and we bring ourselves to drink therefrom in the fullness of trust. This is the ultimate in Loving Intimacy.

"There is another way you can bring yourself into Oneness at the drop of a hat, so to speak. When you are in the company of someone you love, which by now should mean everyone, and you begin to feel disconnected, separate from them, ask if you may link with them. The act of linking is a simple one. Merely take your left hand, the hand that receives, and place it over your own heart. Ask the other person to do likewise, being sure to emphasize that both need to open their heart to the other. Then reach out and touch the other person's heart with your right hand, the hand most associated with giving, placing it over their left hand, instructing them to do likewise with you. Symbolically this ritual does the same thing as the loving draught of spirit exercise. Now just drink to your heart's content of that loving energy that is being transferred from one to another this way. Remember to do this every time you feel disconnected or at odds with another, even if you ask them only to visualize it with you.

"Right now I want you to turn to someone on either side of you and exercise this gifting of unfettered love in exactly this way. Give yourselves a moment to get over your reticence for doing so. Just trust that you can open your heart without someone else abusing it. Trust also that you can receive such healing love from another, even though he or she may be a complete stranger. Breathe, always remember to breathe, and take in the loving energy while at the same time releasing your loving energy to them. Tap into your feelings as you let this transpire. Remember these feelings always, for they can inspire you to repeat this kind of healing any time you wish, either by visualization or in fact."

Christo gives ample time for this loving exercise to take full hold. He sees the arena light up as the loving spirits glow from within each to another. Finally, he inserts: "I suspect that this is a good space in which to take a break. Just sit in the loving embrace you now feel for a few moments and then give yourself some time to digest what we've been dealing with here. If you are able to digest it, then over the next few days you can more fully assimilate it completely into your being. Just remember that whatever has resonated within you personally during this exercise is your inner Truth expressed. It is your inner validation that something very special has spoken to your heart and is to be taken seriously. We'll reconvene in thirty minutes."

As Christo leaves the podium, he sees a sea of Kleenex wiping away tears, tears of tenderness witnessed, and it brings a warm smile to his heart. He will have something to say about expressing love in one's own unique way when he returns.

The Followers, we can now call them, weave their way through the arena, taking mental note of what is happening in the crowd. Conversations are abundant in every direction. Most take on the tone of hushed conversation, almost like innocent embraces of the loving way. Others take on the tone of a grand inquisition, with some arguing and bickering as their witness, but those are few and far between. A closer look, however, finds that most are simply sitting in the reverent silence of their own being. It is obvious that a good bit of savoring is going on. The softness that characterizes those images tells the entire story. Christo takes in the reports from his Followers and sees immediately what he knows to be true about any transition: each person handles it according to where they are in their own spiritual development. He knows, too, that many here, like all throughout existence, would soon, if not already there, become confused. This is a normal function of change, for when we have one foot in a new perspective and one in the old, it is confusing as to which we should we should be standing in at any given moment.

CHAPTER 3

The Simple Life as Image and Likeness of God

Christo sets this understanding aside and goes within to listen for guidance, knowing full well that in the collective consciousness is the answer that needs not even the simplest question to bring Truth forth. Sure enough, in a matter of minutes a knowing smile, rooted in his sacred heart, grows across his face as he lifts himself up from his prayer stool brimming with enthusiasm for the Word. The burning bush of enthusiasm for inner Truth expressed had shown its face once again. He strides toward the podium with a telling spring in his step and the crowd once again comes to a respectful hush, although this time it feels more like a sea of open hearts but still on varying scales of receptivity.

Christo begins as usual: "Namaste, I acknowledge the fullness of God within each of you. I now see that many of you are beginning to acknowledge the same in yourselves, and this is to be applauded. So I want you to take this moment to applaud yourselves for allowing some of your former limiting thoughts about yourselves to go into forgiveness. Join me now, if you will, in that praise you so richly deserve."

Christo begins applauding with great enthusiasm and his appreciative gesture penetrates the atmosphere like a bolt of lightening accompanied by its companion clap of thunder. It startles the crowd at first, resulting in stunned silence. But then, as people begin to understand the celebration of appreciation that Christo has initiated, a few here and there reluctantly join him in applause. Then a few more—and more—and even more. In a matter of seconds, the arena begins to rock with applause, and people are filled with joy in appreciation for what they have come to in such a short time. Such feelings encourage people to feel safe in trusting themselves to go further on this path to inner freedom. The collective consciousness about this is that power-ful—and as Christo knows, inevitable—when people just let the door to Truth's way open even a crack.

He speaks, knowing that the crowd is now ready to penetrate the veil of mystery a good deal more. As usual, his inner Authority has lit the candle with which to enlighten the crowd: "Very soon now you will come to understand that you and God are indeed One and that each of you is a sacred vessel through which God speaks uniquely—just as you were created to be—as the gift to the universe each of you is. Let me illustrate this by using my recollec-tion of one of my favorite television ads. Yes, I know, some of you are thinking, '*You*, watch television?' Well, to tell you the truth, on rare occasions, very rare occasions, I like to touch base to see if anyone can beat Tiger Woods, and once in a great while I do get caught up in advertisements that speak to me. Other than that, I keep away from its distracting quality. Anyhow, my favorite ad to do with the context in which we find ourselves is one marketing 'diamonds are forever.' Envision this with me. Maybe some of you have even seen it.

"The ad begins with this young man and woman strolling through St. Peter's Square, and he is commenting on how joy-filled he feels to be celebrat-ing their anniversary in this special place. He turns to her and says something like, 'I just have to say something, right here, right now,' and she turns her attention in his direction to see what it will be. He takes a stride or two away from her and opens his arms in a wide gesture towards the gods and yells at the top of his voice, 'I LOVE THIS WOMAN! I LOVE HER! I LOVE HER! I LOVE HER! Pigeons scatter everywhere, people's attention is drawn toward them, and the woman cowers in her shyness. He suddenly knows that he has some-what intimidated her and says in a much softer tone, 'All right then, I guess I'll just have to say it this way.' He then pulls out a diamond ring and places it on her finger. Of course, she melts into her shoes. Overtaken by her husband's love for her, she throws her arms around him and whispers ever so softly into the nape of his neck, no less lovingly than her husband had previously declared: '*I love this man. I love him. I love him. I love him.*' A deep expression of love professed, each in one's own unique way.

"I use this story to indicate on the front end that although I will be showing you that you and God are One in being, I want to be clear that by being One with God you do not lose your own individual character. In fact, it is your unique character that God speaks through. Each who crosses your path hears loving expressed in the way that speaks only to them, so they need the variation that is you in order for that resonance with love to be heard at the deepest level. With that understanding as a basis, I hope you will let any fear of losing yourself go, at least as you have come to understand it to this point."

Christo pauses for a moment, turning his head to one side, as though needing to hear what someone was saying to him. He smiles knowingly and then resumes.

"Well, let me take this one step further, for it comes to me that this might still be confusing to some. Let's reframe the idea of losing yourself before seeing what self really means. When it is said that you must lose yourself in order to find God, that doesn't for a moment mean that you are to lose your essence, the essential character God created you to be. That would be impossible. Neither does it mean that you would lose your individual character. What losing oneself really means is that each of us must get out of our own self-importance in order to serve a higher purpose than fulfillment of our ego, our false self, and our thoughts that we are the center of the universe.

"When we get out of our own way, so to speak, the flow of loving energy, God by another name, is freed to energize any who come our way. Because each of us is a uniquely designed character, that loving energy flows through us in that individual form: some loud and clear, very much like the man in the ad; some soft and just as clear, like the woman in the ad; and everything in between. In short, then, it is very important that each of us has a unique character so that all can be spoken to, served, in a way that speaks uniquely to them. And there you have it. Now, let's continue on today's journey of coming to see how God and we are One.

"I can learn to understand myself somewhat through my human intellect, yet I can understand myself in an even more profound sense through a deeper level of awareness: a spiritual knowing that is filled with the offerings of insight and contained in divine wisdom. This knowing can be found only in our relationship between God and ourselves, and with God in all else. I love the way the Persian poet, Hafiz, awakens us to this need to dive to the depths, beyond intellectual expression:

Someone Should Start Laughing

I have a thousand brilliant lies
For the question
How are you?

I have a thousand brilliant lies
For the question
What is God?

If you think that the Truth can be known
From words,
If you think that the Sun and the Ocean
Can pass through that tiny opening
Called the mouth,
O someone should start laughing!
Someone should start wildly Laughing—
Now!

"For most of us, we think we know and understand the words that are used to describe God, as in infinite God, immortal God, life, love, spirit, and soul. Yet how can we really know the meanings of 'infinite,' 'immortal,' 'perfect' in the deeper sense of these terms? These are terms defined by some outside authority, and we already are coming to understand that in order to truly understand anything we must go within to satisfy our wonder. It is in the spiritual sense of innocence that we must come to know real meaning, for in the mortal sense, the intellect, reality simply is not. The intellect by itself is too limiting for our purposes of spiritual discernment. But the intellect can be a threshold for us to initiate the eventual spiritual understanding. In actuality, we all are at different levels of understanding, and all levels feed into still others as long as we stay the course, persist in our quest for the Ultimate in meaning. The teachings of Jesus are about the Spirit of Loving. Thus their meaning must, it seems to me, be discerned by a means beyond the intellect, namely through the symbolic or metaphorical tongue in which Jesus spoke.

"Actually, it is the quest itself that is the living of the Loving Spirit. Somewhere down deep in the soul of our fiber we already know we are Loving, expressing in the image and likeness of God. It is just that we forget that we are, mostly because we love mostly only superficially. When we love through our immature, externally provoked thoughts only, the best we can do is become infatuated with others and things. We skim the surface and find in a very short time that we have lost interest in that with which we are infatuated. On the other hand, when we re-member with authentic Loving, which comes only by engaging life from the depths of our heart, we enfold life with unfathomable enthusiasm, indeed, in a Spirit of Loving-kindness for Life itself, and for all we choose to engage along the way.

"As we listen to God as our way of praying, it is in this sacred space, free from our own inane thoughts, that we empty ourselves to hear the 'still small voice within.' This prompts discernment of God's True meaning, Spiritual meaning, for us. We all know it when it appears. This takes us a big step beyond the intellectual meaning—to inner meaning—the meaning that comes from innocence delivered. It is only then that we can have an appropriate frame of reference or a set of lenses through which we can view the demonstration of God on this journey we call Life. This is a most powerful means of discerning Truth. Unfortunately, however, most of us have not yet been prepared to fathom the depths of Soul this way. We must take care to avail ourselves of the opportunities to establish such skills and persist on this pathway toward enlightenment.

"One last admonition, a powerful reminder of our true Essence of Being, lest we perpetuate the view of God all too many of us hold to be true: a god created all too often in our own tarnished image. This comes from another Persian poet, Rumi:

You think of yourself
as a citizen of the universe.
You think you belong
to this world of dust and matter.
Out of this dust
you have created a personal image,
and have forgotten
about the essence of your true origin.

"The Master Jesus tells us essentially the same thing many times and in many ways, yet we still insist on mirroring ourselves into the face of God, rather than the other way around. Our individual process is ours to discern.

Until we define that spiritual path for ourselves and fervently commit to it, thinly disguised efforts at knowing and demonstrating our sacred reality will fall on fallow ground. We remain a house divided against itself."

Christo once again scans the crowd in tandem with his inner Authority, and he is confident that they are largely in harmony. He is acting much like a bird building a nest, just following his inner callings moment by moment in order to bring to the nest what serves it best. The nest in this case, of course, is that which is needed for the spirit to be at home in each instance.

"Well, then," Christo continues, "it seems to me that before you can see how you and God are one, you had better understand what you *are*. Unfortunately, in this material world of thought in which we find ourselves, but not *of* it I must add, we mostly speak of *who* we are, such importance do most give to the roles we play. We ask of one another, 'Who are you?' That is quickly followed by, 'And what do you do?' When we have answered those questions, the space between the real you and what you do disappears into the role in which you have placed yourself, and each of us becomes a label: housewife, painter, electrician, lover, or whatever. These represent who we say we are.

"The moment we accept a label, we are separated from all others, for we are pointed to as being someone 'out there, separate from me, who does this or that.' Separation has thus been established, and there is only one way around it: to reestablish oneness to its original form, as the Truth of life. 'How on earth can we do that?' you ask. Let's dream about it together for a moment.

"'Who' is a word that defines role. 'What,' on the other hand, defines the essence of being. Let me test this by asking you this question, and I want you to make a mental note to remember the first answer you give, without thinking about it; the first thought you have in reaction to the question. Here it is: 'What are you?'"

Christo pauses and lets people record their answers. Then he resumes: "Now, how many of you responded with something like housewife, carpenter, writer, teacher, lawyer? Raise your hand if you did so." Almost everyone in the arena raises a hand. "Ha! I told you so!" exclaims Christo. "This shows you how strongly you have been brainwashed inito believing that you are defined by what you do rather than what you really are. When we allow ourselves to be defined with a label of role attached, then we are separating ourselves further from those around us who judge us by letting us know—whether or not we want to know—how well we are performing that role. It establishes a distance from one another that provides just enough separation to point a finger at us in judgment of our performance.

"Whenever we point outside of ourselves we establish separation, period, and in so doing both we and others establish expectations for our roles. And then we set ourselves up to try to meet all these expectations. Then we get our underwear all tied up in knots over how well we are meeting them and more often than not look for outside validation, rather than relying on our own internal sense of self to validate our goodness. Is it any wonder that from the outside we must look as though we're paranoid?

"Now, close your eyes for a moment and take yourselves as far as you can into silence. Breathe deeply, slowly. Watch your current thoughts go by without judgment."

Christo feels the collective energy propel the crowd into receptive space very quickly, so he continues with his penetrating directions: "Now, dismiss yourself from any role you now play, letting it float away, wherever it wishes to go. If it is helpful, paste a label on an image of yourself and attach it to a huge balloon and then let it float away. Don't be scared, this is only a vision, and you'll still be here as you are when we are finished. Trust me just a few moments more in this exercise. Sit now in this vacuous space, and hear this question in the seat of your heart, not the pit of your mind. Come from intuition, not analytical intellect. Remember the first thing that comes up from deep within. Ready? The question is this: 'WHAT are you?'"

Once again Christo gives them time but not for reflection, for reflection would create too much logical application. He allows time for the answer that can come only from the immediacy of intuition or instinct. He senses in the flash of the moment that the point has struck home, deep in the soul level of most. "Okay, how many of you heard something like this come up from your deepest self? I am the essence of God, or I am a child, a creation of God. Or I am God's idea of me expressed, or anything akin to these?" Most of the hands in the crowd shoot up, enthusiastically even.

"Greatness!" reinforces Christo. "Now you're coming to your senses, your real senses. When you can sense that you and God are of the same loving essence, you have just reunited in Oneness, re-membered with it, and separation and duality have vanished as possibilities. The Truth of the matter is that the only matter is the Essence of the Loving Spirit. If this were not so, then we would have to give up the Truth that God is everywhere present, ever potent, ever knowing, and ever active. But because these spiritual laws are the only true laws of the spiritual life to which we eternally belong, then we must conclude that we, too, are of this same Essence called the Loving Way. In Truth, it is what we are and only what we are to express. Anything else that we think or do is only a figment of our imagination that comes to the fore when we are fearful or forgetful, and this is so about each of us. Anything to the contrary to what we really are is only an illusion we create in opposition to that. This is the feeling of separation that keeps driving us in a direction away from Oneness, the empty feeling we get from the world outside our deepest, inner self.

"We get this feeling from what we are told by some in our churches. For example, we hear that only God is holy—that only God is powerful—and that God is in Heaven and we on earth. These are all projections of separateness. We also get this feeling because the advertising and marketing industry has established in our minds that we are separate, or different, which they would like us to think are the same, so they can sell the products that make us feel on the outside that we are just like this or that illusory entity. Again, this reinforces the concept of separation and duality, them and us, which becomes us *versus* them over the long haul. This establishes the rule of competition over the Truth of collaboration. On and on this insidious game goes, until and unless we come to the understanding that the only way to win that zero sum game of competition is not to play it at all.

"Instead, we can retreat into the Truth of our loving Oneness, and the compassionate expression of the Essence of which we all are a necessary part. Then validation of our True value comes about not from external validation, but from the answer to one simple question we ask within: 'Am I behaving lovingly, in and through all I do?' The only evaluation necessary can then be met with a simple 'yes' or 'no.' Either we are creating life—our thoughts about life—lovingly or we are not. There is no part way, no badly, no fairly well, no grandly. A simple 'yes' or 'no' will do. Then another question can be asked if we are not behaving lovingly: 'What can I do to change my demonstration to one that is lovingly expressed?' Asking these two questions within will provide all the Truth we need to live a fulfilled life. All around us will benefit likewise by our obedience to this Loving principle.

"All benefit when we create life lovingly as a lawyer, a housewife, a carpenter, an artist, a teacher, a friend, or a lover. We simply demonstrate our loving-kindness through all we are and do. What a simple life this becomes when we strip away all the impediments to freely expressing the loving essence we really are, instead of trying to impress our ego and others in some competitive expression or another. Expressing what we really are to others who reside in their own Godliness instantaneously creates Oneness. Trying to meet irrelevant expectations that have nothing whatsoever to do with loving creation only separates us from others and even the reality of our spiritual being.

"No wonder our thoughts are a house divided against itself. The house in this case is expressed as our container of consciousness. The question becomes how and to where we consciously express life, our thoughts: lovingly or not? Is it from within or without? When we place ourselves in a position to look outside ourselves for God, for the answers we need to live by and for validation of our inherent worth, we are consciously expressing to false gods. When we instead we go within for all these, for all we need in order to express a life filled with peace of mind and a joy-filled heart, we are consciously expressing our most natural state of being. When we go inward we establish our lives on the impenetrable foundation of God-reliance, which is our absolute sufficiency. On the other hand, when we go without, we substantiate self-reliance, which is nothing but an illusional figment of egocentricity and a reflection of hubris, the ultimate of arrogance expressed. Again, we live by choice: am I consciously expressing my authentic self or a mere facsimile constructed by using sources outside what I really am?

"I can feel that you are well on your way to seeing yourselves as a necessary part of a larger whole, the whole universe of Loving Essence. Also, it wouldn't surprise me if you hadn't quite yet accepted this Truth, or weren't at least a bit confused about how this would work in your day-to-day world. So, let's take a leap of faith together. I think you're ready to move beyond the inch-by-inch approach and consider a major change in how you actually relate to the God that resides within each of you, and thus one another. I'd like to do this by starting in a place of old, that being with a literal translation of the characteristics attributed to God, and then leaping to a more spiritual translation of it that will unite you with God in the resonance of its Truth for you. Come with me and you will see what I mean very quickly, for you are now ready for the leap of faith. Rest assured that for each of you, when you leap God will either catch you if your falter or teach you how to fly."

A sudden restful realization seems to captivate the crowd as a surge of reassuring energy courses through their midst in affirming measure.

"I want you to understand that you will not necessarily see the wisdom of what is to come all at once, although some might. For most, understanding needs curing in order to become wisdom. So many of us are in such a hurry to become this or that, to achieve a certain level as soon as we can. That's a form of immediate gratification that permeates our culture. We must remember that one cannot force God to meet our puny view of life, no more than you can force the bloom of a rose without destroying its natural intention or giftedness. The richness of the Truth of any of God's gifts can be found only by letting them mature through their own natural curative process, each in its own time. Healing results when we come to enlightenment about a certain misperceived idea or belief. The cure takes its own time to show up in material form.

"Living in this understanding is what Jesus meant when he said that we should become like children. Obviously he didn't mean we should be childish, but rather that we should return to the innocence from which flows a natural basis of loving. Even though young children get knocked away from that foundation by momentary distractions in the outer world, instinctively they return to their loving foundation quickly. A child may fight with a playmate one minute then embrace him the next. Innocence in this context means that a child moves from moment to moment directed by what seems like some mysterious authority. A child moves from this toy to that: being amused by specks of dust dancing in the sunlit window; rolling over and being nourished by the oral stimulation of thumb in mouth; reaching out for a warm milk bottle; letting trapped gas pass unadorned by pride. In each instance, the child is acting in obedience to inner guidance, unaffected by external demands, unlimited by concern for external judgment applied by the unknowing.

"This can happen in young children because they have not yet been contaminated by the vagaries of domestication. They can feel the deepest resonance with their inner Authority just as easily as they can play with and express their feelings. They giggle when reaching for the specks of dust dancing in the ray of light; emit the 'hmm' sound of satisfaction from a thumb sucked; grunt or let a slight wail out when the trapped gas emits. Youngsters know exactly how they feel, and they don't think the feelings are what they are; they just feel them and move on to the next moment. This is the childlike innocence of which Jesus spoke. This is the innocence that Jesus beckons us to return to, so we can live True to ourselves moment by loving moment and not get trapped in the failings of the domestication process that have wounded us all. Children are like wet cement: anything that falls on them makes an impression. But they only acknowledge the impression and move on. Adults are like dry cement: all mixed up and hardened. What falls on us bounces us around and upsets our equilibrium until we can figure out that there's another way to deal with life: out of childlike innocence.

"If this seems like an unlikely pattern for adults to follow, let me give you another example, one used by Jesus in which he simplifies it even more. At first blush this, too, might seem like an unlikely act for us to emulate, but in your increased ability to apply it metaphorically, I am confident you will see the wisdom in it almost immediately. Once again, close your eyes for a moment and rest in the stillness of your heart. Take a few slow, deep breaths to clear out the tension from the area around your heart. Take a stretch or two to expand the possibility for clearing muscle tension. Breathe refreshing expanses of air into places of your musculature that seem tense to you. Take your time."

Christo pauses to give everyone time to come to a space of receptivity for absorbing this next layer of spiritual imagery: "Okay, now I want you to let your thoughts pass before your inner eyes and just notice what they are informing you about. Don't latch onto the thoughts. You might just want to make a mental note so they can be assured you will scan them for any importance later on. Notice as you do this that fewer and fewer appear. Very soon now you will come to a space where you are anticipating the next thought, but none appears.

"When you reach this space within you, let yourself envision a bird, any bird that you happen to like. It really doesn't matter what kind. Now watch it build a nest...and where it has initiated this natural expression of creativity...Latch onto it and ride with it as it goes about its business...Simply watch, don't direct it in any way...Make a mental note of its actions, not judging it according to what you think about the actions or want the bird to do, but simply as an observer of the process...All right, when the bird has completed the task, recollect the path it chose to do so...Now compare its methodology to that you would use to accomplish a similar task...Make a simple declaration about whether you and the bird have used the same process. A simple 'yes' or 'no' will do...With a raise of the hands, how many of you recorded a simple 'no way' in answer to that last question?" The vast majority of the crowd raises a hand. "Ahah! Caught you, didn't I?" Christo challenges them laughingly.

"Let's take a look at what you saw. Let me describe it, for the collective consciousness painted this picture in my mind's eye from the perspective of the bird. The bird found a piece of string and took it to the fledgling bed of a nest. It looked at it for a moment and then flew off in another direction, alighting on a birdbath alongside an adjoining garden. Bathing for a few moments, the bird is chased away by a larger one and scurries away to a neighboring windowsill where it proceeds to clean itself, pecking under its wings, then at its hindquarter. Shortly the bird flies away, snatching a bug in its beak, landing on a limb nearby to savor its catch. Seeing another useful twig nearby, the bird swoops down to fetch it in its beak and then proceeds to feather its bed one more time. On and on the bird goes, in this seemingly erratic, disorganized pattern. Yet, by the end of the day, the bird has not only fulfilled its major purpose of building the nest it needs, it has also met all its various other needs along the way. Each moment was seemingly guided by some mysterious wisdom, although it appeared on the surface that this was not the case. And you can be assured that along the way the bird did not worry about a single thing while it was responding only to each momentary need.

"This is the path that the Master Jesus indicated for us to travel upon. Think about it for just another moment with me, please. Did the bird have some master plan in its mind when it started out the day? Hardly, it had just a single purpose in the end. Do you think that it had a set of goals to achieve? Hardly. Do you think it had established any expectations that might have frustrated it if they hadn't been met by the end of the day? Nope. Do you think it had any concern about anything or anyone along the way? No way. All it did was respond to the simplest direction from within, everything else be damned. Now this is the simple life.

"Can we as humans live profitably this way? You may doubt it, but I am here to assure you that we are intended to live only in *exactly* this way. It is mankind's image of competition and fear of lack that keeps us in a frenetic pace of life. When we take time to slow down and listen within, our life becomes much simpler, and we live according to our inner prompting only. The result? We find that we are living a blessed life and that our every need is taken care of. We find that we know what we must do is completed not only when it must be, but exactly how it must be. And we find that it all seems to come about by grace, as presents that somehow show up moment by moment. Indeed, this is grace that is our sufficiency in all matters. It is what comes out of living from our innocence and trusting that to be our only valid choice. When we grow to trust the validity of this approach, we suddenly realize that we feel fulfilled each day. We have a sense of contributing to life. We find that our relationships are lovingly intimate on all levels of Being. Let's hear it for innocence!

"I apologize for what may seem to you like a meandering way to your likeness with God, but there is a force at work here that doesn't meet our seeming need for rational direction. Truth works in a way that informs each of us about the proper road for us to take moment by moment. I am following that road exactly as I am being directed to do so. When I have been impatient so as to apply another direction, I am led to take a path of corrective measure. Ego needs are what have displayed themselves as the road meanders. So be patient with me in my human nature, and you will come to see how this is indeed beneficial in the long run, which, by the way, is the single criterion with which to judge success for each of us.

"All of you have heard that God made it all and called it good. This could well lead us to determine that God was named from his goodness. We also have heard God spoken of as the Supreme Being, Jehovah, the eternal and infinite spirit, the creator, the sovereign of the universe, and more. As long as we take these descriptors of God as something apart from ourselves, we have created a distancing of ourselves from God, a stamp of separation that colors the way we see ourselves in relationship with all of life. All of life becomes something that is, and happens, 'out there' somewhere. The real keys of understanding, however, unlock this darkened door of duality.

"If we understand that the Essence of God is everywhere present, and all powerful, and all knowing, and constantly active, then we come to further understand that there can be no room for anything of its opposite. As a matter of fact, opposite cannot exist in a world filled with nothing but God. Duality is thus eliminated in this Omnipresence of God. God, as the expression of Loving Spirit, is everywhere present, so there is no place for anything else to be present. Two things cannot occupy the same space. It falls to the understanding, then, that there is nothing else but God, by whatever name. This being so, there also is no opposite to the characteristics of God. No duality possible. There is only what Is—and that is God, by whatever term. All else is mankind's illusion, a figment of one's imagination, or in this case, a collective figment perpetrated by the need for rational, intellectual determination in any given situation. You will recall the reference to this illusion in the Adam and Eve story. Simply put, mankind creates only counterfeit illusion to cope with its ego demands. Living this new understanding eliminates the need for dualities and places total emphasis and importance on the One in Being, and each of us the same, as the Essence of God each of us is. Separateness disappears in its wake, as does the pain that corroborates the feeling of separation.

"Thus, when we begin dismissing the old, worn-out, contrary illusions about who we think we are and eventually come to appreciate and live what we really Are, we bathe in the revelation of Truth. Instead of trying to cope with the other-directed demands and expectations inserted into our psyche through the process of domestication, perhaps even in prenatal form, we find ourselves in a state of Grace. Both our woundedness and the need for forgiveness are rendered unnecessary in the wake of understanding this new information about God and us.

"Only mankind creates thoughts opposite to Good, or God, all in the illusions of a sick mind. Only mankind creates the illusions of bad, ugly, sin, disease, and death. Good is all there Is: God fills all space with Its goodness—and we, as the perfect image of God, also are the perfect demonstration of Goodness. In this way, we also come to see that behind every human or mortal mask is the face of God. We just need to reinterpret or recast, reframe, our human mask, our thoughts about it, as the face of God. Then perfection, yours and mine, is reinstated. We don't have to learn perfection or earn it; we already *are* it, always have been, are, and will be. There's nothing to become, only veils of illusion to rend. So whenever we take on a form of thinking that places us in the realm of who we have come to believe we are, perhaps out of what a parent or sibling has labeled us under some dire circumstances, we can now make a choice to choose something else as our self-image—a choice to think of ourselves as the reality of goodness we are and nothing else.

"We can rightfully be led to see that God is spirit; life; ardor; fire; courage; elevation or vehemence of mind; an immaterial intelligent substance; and the soul of humankind. We, too, are spirit, or spiritual beings. Thus, we, too, are of life. We, too, are ardor; courage; immaterial intelligent substance and the soul of humankind. We exhibit life when we let our creative juices flow, creating lovingly at every opportunity. We exhibit ardor when we unleash burning desire and unbridled enthusiasm for our given purpose in life. We exhibit courage every time we look fear in the eye and move through the fear to loving creativity on the other side. We are immaterial, intelligent substance every time we get out of our own controlling ways and let God work through us. We are the soul of humankind, in likeness with all others, when we open ourselves fully to another in celebration of the gift life is. Yes, we are of a much higher vibration and more sacred substance than we have ever given ourselves credit for being—and we exhibit it much more readily and frequently than we give ourselves credit for having done so. The only thing standing between the realization of this elevated Being and our present demonstration is self-imposed fear and limitation. It's all in the way we think about ourselves. As we begin to replace shopworn illusions with our Truth, we more and more reflect that Truth rather than illusory, fear-related pictures of ourselves, those images imposed either from within or without.

"God is the Permanent Being, Eternal, without beginning or ending of existence. Thus, we, too, as spiritual beings, must be so: permanent, eternal, without beginning or ending of existence. It is we who insert the contrary concept of linear, rational mortality—and its necessary companion: death. But, as Eternal beings, death is defeated, obliterated from our belief system, eradicated from possibility. As spiritual beings there is only eternity, not death. Our physical body may disintegrate, but our spirit lives on. To the degree that we have made the transition to this new understanding of our immortality, our process of saging will be unlimited by time and place. In our space together this afternoon, time has ceased to exist. Not one of you has looked at your watch while we have been engaged in one another. Time has seemed to stand still. This is eternity defined. Engaging life presently *is* eternity.

"God's perfection is also infinite, as is Its presence. We, too, when stripped from our self-inflicted limitations, are infinite in our perfection and in our presence. We are perfect when we live what we are and go within to Truth for direction and then obey it without fail. We are perfect when we exhibit Loving as our way of life. In order to arrive at this new understanding, all we have to do is dismiss the limitations of the contrary belief system we have absorbed and manifested in thought and deed, and we are freed to be limitless, eternal and immortal in our perfection and presence. We thus have no perfection or presence to achieve. In the sacredness of our being, we simply *are* Perfection and Presence—as well as Presents. We always have been and always will be That. Therefore, we do not have to achieve what we already Are: we already *are* It. We just need to Be It in order to demonstrate what we Are. We simply need to demonstrate our Perfection by being whole and ever-Present in each moment of this gift called Life.

"As we think about our relationship with God we must remind ourselves that it reflects Oneness in spirit, not material physicality. So when we say that God is omniscient, omnipotent, omni-present and omni-active, we are speaking of the ineffable Essence of God in spiritual existence. Therefore, when we are One with God, and have been created in God's image and likeness, this, too, means spiritually, not physically. By extension, then, as we tap into our Truth within, we are all-knowing, for there is no spiritual answer that is unavailable in the Universe's storehouse of wisdom when we wonder within. Wonder unleashes Innocence as Truth through us, and we are to follow its beckoning call obediently. As it is with God, omniscience is also our way.

"By expressing our nature of loving creativity, we are omnipotent, for the strength of God's Loving ways is unmistakably all powerful. The power of it can move mountains of difference; it can turn hate into love; it can heal the infirmed; make the blind to see; the deaf to hear; even raise the dead. What could be more powerful in the spiritual world?

"And omnipresence, what of it? In our transcendent form of existence, we are everywhere present because we have come to understand that our Spirit and the Spirit of God are One, and if indeed God is everywhere present, so must we be. In our mind's eye, we can and do go anywhere Spirit can go, for as part of the Universal Consciousness, there is no place Spirit, and therefore we, are not.

"We are omni-active in the sense that Spirit never ceases to work for us. Awake or asleep, our connection to Soul continuously works on our behalf to see that our highest good is being fulfilled. Even when we seemingly leave presence, Spirit is working on our behalf, forever tapping into the universe of ideas in order to serve what is best for us, despite our frequent efforts to the contrary. Even in the physical realm we are expressing omni-action, for our organs, blood stream, flow of air, and intake and processing of images of all kinds never ceases. Yes, even in these ways, contrary to those who think only in physical terms, we are One with God.

"All of this is the Essence of Intimacy, the authentic presentation of exactly what we really are to the entirety of our existence; presenting ourselves in the understanding that we are holy and sacred in our humanness. This, too, is our perfection. This is what the life of Jesus taught us. All we need do is accept this as our Truth and live it thus. Indeed, we will come to demonstrate our new-found True Nature most naturally to the exact degree we can think and accept this Truth about ourSelves. This is exactly what Jesus was teaching us through the example of his own life. Unfortunately, however, this has been countered so arduously by the example of the loveless thought images perpetrated and perpetuated by others who gain by our thoughts, just as they would have us do.

"When we allow ourselves the grace of such understanding in our day-to-day lives, when we exercise or demonstrate unencumbered Presence, we are Perfect in our Being with another. We find the ultimate, Loving, expressed as Loving Spirit, or Eros, with a capital E. Eros, the sacred depths of Loving, is a form of Loving that is so deep and so profound as to render it indefinable in words. This desire for Union with God is extraordinary in its Effect because it fathoms much deeper and richer than any mortal feeling can assimilate or interpret. It can be lived in each moment when we eliminate the resistance in our thought barriers, those illusions that have prevented us from witnessing even a glimpse of real Loving in our past.

"Now is a different understanding and demonstration possible, stripped of the illusions, these errors in thinking that have heretofore clouded or veiled the Truth of Loving's real existence. The fact of the matter is that real Loving has always existed. It is we who have not heard its knock on the door of our inner Being. It is we who have looked for it elsewhere, outside of ourselves, instead of simply Being the Loving Essence we, ourselves, are, in all its fullness. In contrast, what we most often find outside of ourselves are various forms of substitutes or counterfeits for the Loving Essence we truly are. These substitutes are nothing less than our infatuations personified. As we engage in relationship with others we just need to remember that infatuation in a superficial, short-lived impression of the intellect upon the material. Infatuation has nothing whatsoever to say about how Loving Spirit transforms and transcends the superficial through Ultimate Intimacy exchanged.

"I momentarily divert once again to insert a slightly different tack, another perspective of God, a reframing of our thinking, if you will. As we depart on our journey to discern the various aspects or characterizations of God, then, it would seem wise to remember that they represent the demonstrations of the Father-Mother God. By that I mean we do ourselves good by investigating the feminine and masculine characteristics of behavior united in each of us, as the complete Ideas of God we are. It is only when we acknowledge both aspects, heretofore thought by many to be only separately possessed by either man or woman, that we come into balance—are rendered complete—in our Oneness as reflections of God.

"We can note from Scripture that the Truth of creation is that man and woman were one idea, one creation, both in One. Thus is our internal, our Spiritual weddedness with God of which Jesus spoke. We are as God Is, thus complete in our Father-Motherness, and demonstrate this as the awakened Beings we Are, in the Loving ways we engage life. For some, this will be a first, albeit a perhaps reluctant, awakening to this Truth. For all, eventually it is the realization, to the degree we are aware, that we demonstrate all these character-istics quite instinctively. We all are, at our core, the reflection or image, and the likeness of God, the divine Idea of Father-Mother that is complete in each of us. It remains unclear only to the degree that we resist or disown this Truth about ourselves. When we find ourselves in a state of confusion about this it is primarily because we have one foot still in our past understanding, while the other is resting firmly in the new, and an internal tug of war shows itself as confusion. We say 'I don't know' when asked how what we think about such things, when what we really in truth ought to be confessing is that we simply are confused and need a little more time and information for the curative pro-cess to show the way.

"When we do resist or disown over a long duration, for example, we reflect some aberration of Truth, rather than the reality of Truth that balances us, that renders us whole, and that puts us fully at ease with all aspects of our Loving selves. When we disown a particular facet of our capability, either good or not so good, we reflect in Truth's wake a part of our shadow self, which most often manifests as some addiction to a perverted or unlike image of our realty as spiritual, Loving Essence. It is also true that unless we come in contact with that inner erroneous image it is likely to maintain it as that described, or come to loom even larger in our everyday lives. The only helpful response is to use these images as opportunities for discovering the Truth about what we have disowned in relation to own behavior and beliefs.

"Perhaps a personal example will help. Not too long ago I had the opportunity to work with someone with a very large ego. My intuition said that it would not be good for me to do so, but I didn't listen to the word in this instance, because I rationalized that it would be worth the risk for the sake of the income potential. Well, it didn't take too long for me to get highly irritated by the various abusive expressions of ego by this person. In the end I had to come to grips with why I was being so irritated by his actions. The more obvious reason was that it didn't feel good to be violated in this fashion. The less obvious was that I had failed to see in the beginning that I had disowned my own ego in making the decision I had. How? By putting myself in a position to be diminished, and by rationalizing that some amount of money could make up for it. Finally I came to the ultimate Truth for me in this situation: For just how much am I willing to sell my self-respect? As usual, the answer was found in the question when I let intuition speak once again instead of unabashed ego need: my self-respect is not for sale at any price. Additionally I came to realize that I ought not to place myself in the company or any circumstance that belittles me, that makes me feel little rather than expansive. Thank God for the loan of this person, so I could learn these lessons at last.

"Let us explore this revelation of the Father-Mother God a bit further. In our society, in fact in most of the world as we know it today, our mortal sense of being, shaped in this case by our beliefs in separateness from God and one another as well as in gender difference, would tell us that each of us is either male or female in gender. We are different and separate, apart, so such thinking tells us. It tells us that perhaps one is even better than the other, or that we therefore need someone of the opposite gender to complete us.

"In same gender relationships it is no different, for on the outside at least, one of the partners generally demonstrates the more masculine characteristics and the other the more feminine characteristics. Thus when we, either as a male or female, fail to acknowledge the balance of both the divine feminine and masculine within ourselves, in the image of the divine Father-Mother we are, we somehow feel empty, incomplete, and we look outside ourselves for completion. This is neither bad nor good. It merely is what it is. Just know that until we assimilate this awareness of the inner-balanced being, we will feel separate from the supposed opposite gender. Perhaps the other arrives in our midst to teach us what is really needed, from the inside, to be complete. In the final analysis, it is each of us, and not the other, who can and must complete oneself in this understanding and all its manifestations. Thus we find that we don't need another to complete us at all. Instead, we come to understand that what we really desire is someone with whom to safely share our completeness.

"Any form of such aberrant thinking that creates separateness is in error: we already *are* complete, always have been, and always will be. We have just been domesticated to believe otherwise. We have been led to believe we are what others, all others, have, in one way or another, wanted us to be—unless, of course, we have been ever vigilant in keeping such false options away from our spiritual door. Our families, peers, and friends and enemies alike have regularly reinforced this kind of thinking. As children, we may not have been able to be so vigilant in defending against such erroneous assaults. As adults, however, we can now be more discerning and take a stand for what we really are and want so fervently therefore to express. We can reshape the errors of our past into our Truths for today.

"We can reshape our thinking to reflect new understandings, refilling our minds with more loving thoughts than heretofore. As we commit to doing so we come to understand and know with conviction, and more readily demonstrate, all the traits of the Father-Mother God: the tender, nourishing, loving, beauty, sweetness, purity, innocence and spiritual bliss of the feminine; and the life, strength, pure consciousness, spiritual understanding, vitality and vigor of the masculine. Think of these characteristics for just a moment. How many of you, both men and women, regularly exhibit the characteristics attributed to the masculine demonstration of God? Raise your hand high and mighty." Every single hand goes up, without hesitation. "Good for you! Now, think of the characteristics attributed to the feminine aspects of God. Either as a man or woman, raise your hand high and mighty if you regularly exhibit these characteristics." Again, every hand reaches high to the sky.

It is becoming more and more apparent that the crowd is beginning to see the reality of their similarity to God. Living in the image and likeness of God is taking on new meaning for them. Again Christo champions their growing awareness: "Now that's clarity! The more wholesomely you come to this understanding of being in the image and likeness of God the more inner balance you will exhibit, the more complete you will feel, and the more freedom you will find to just be yourself, instead of thinking you have to look for something or someone outside yourself to complete you.

"All the rational, materialistic neediness to become complete from outside ourselves falls aside in favor of the inner knowing of Completeness. We come to be at One within ourselves, reflecting the Completeness of our Father-Mother God. Indeed, we are finally at home in ourSelves, the complete, whole beings of Loving each of us is. A highly important wedding bond, a spiritual re-membering with our completeness, is also rendered. We thus have a new foundation from which loving our neighbors as ourselves becomes a reality. As a result, when an interiorly whole person meets another of like Spirit, the relationship becomes not one of completing one another, but rather one of celebrating the Eros that transpires within and between the amalgam of the completed entities: God with the son and daughter of God, children all, in the depths of Loving energy, the Essence of Eros, the ultimate in Love expressed in the Completeness each one Is.

"This is a celebration of the revelation of non-duality; the disappearance of the division of gender difference when seen in the light of its Oneness. Gender difference is an all too commonly held astigmatism, a distortion in our vision. It is a focus warp that blinds us from Reality. This error in thinking that is its illusory cause is replaced by the Truth of Life and Loving—and we are healed by understanding that God is the only cause—and only effect—in this case, Loving. Loving produces, is only, Loving, and cannot produce anything but what it Is. In all Reality then, there is only Oneness; thus cause and effect are one in the same. The effect is contained in the cause, just as any answer is contained in the question that elicits it. We finally find ourselves in a state divine Loving, as a body and in a pace of Loving that fills us to overflowing, which can be shared with unabashed lavishness in various forms, not the least of which is compassion for our planetary partners.

"Why put ourselves through all this realignment of thought? Don't panic, you don't have to do it all in one large bite. What's important is to imbed the *process* in your heart, so that over time you can use Truth as your only guide to loving perspectives. What's important to understand is that it is the *process* that becomes the Heaven we endlessly seek, and not the end product itself. Loving is the Truth *and the way*, remember. It is only by continually reframing our ideas and beliefs that we heal the ills caused by aligning our thinking with concepts relating to lives of separation, that which cripples us when we subscribe to such thinking.

"Let's take just a moment to reflect on how different our relationships are going to be now that we are able to enter them as complete beings rather than holding others hostage in hopes that they are going to complete us—and then, inevitably, being disappointed and hostile towards them because they didn't do what they simply could not. When we work within ourselves for such changes and then serve as a bridge for others to do likewise, then we come to behave as Jesus did. Jesus did this for all who wanted what he had to offer. We, as awakened beings, can do no less for one another.

"In sum, as we let ourselves simply Be we reframe our vision to see that these aforementioned qualities of God are also the essential qualities of our Being, something eminently pure and refined. In our marvelously renewed nature we are thus redeemed by the influences of the Holy Spirit, rendered in its clearest understanding and demonstration. Clear thinking is our common link to Jesus and the God of Loving that spoke through him. Thus it becomes the same God of Loving that speaks through us. Such a realization forms the foundation for recreating our new theological mythology of Jesus, and thus ourselves, in that image and likeness.

"If we were to review descriptors for loving from our position of base mortality, we would demean Love in its sacred sense. But when we eliminate this erroneous approach from being, we find Loving to be affection expressed, simple and compound; gratitude; delight; happiness; benevolence; the sum of all excellence; excited by beauty and worth of any kind. Loving is expressed in kindness; ardent friendship; charity; patriotism; good will; endearment; civility; instinct; compassion; esteem and reverence conveyed; qualities that render social intercourse agreeable. We find It expressed as excellencies of character, which afford the deepest delight to the sanctified heart.

"Translated into a more definitive expression, Loving demonstrates something like this. The act of Loving moves back and forth between simply a favored disposition and Erotic Passion, depending on circumstances. Eros, as used here, with an uppercase E, means the deepest, most profound form of Passion: Passion of the divine Spirit coursing through us. It is distinct from human passion, the usual mortal display often misinterpreted as raw sexual desire, or eros, with a lowercase e, often demonstrated in relationships powered by infatuation rather than the depths of mature love. The former displays in the awakened Passion for life itself, one who lives all one does with Passion, not simply expressing passion in relationship with one's partner. Loving expresses as gratitude, a virtue of the highest order, as it implies a feeling of a generous heart and a proper sense of duty; an agreeable emotion based on a good feeling and good will toward a benefactor. It manifests in giving or affording high satisfaction or joy. Loving expresses itself as happiness, the enjoyment of peace of mind, of peace within, being at home with what we already are. Raise your hand if you have displayed any of these loving forms." Again, the entire body raises their hands high and proud. "Of course you have! Wonderful! Just *know* that you are demonstrating in the same ways as does God. Actually, it is Loving demonstrating in Its highest accord, with us as the vehicle. It's Eros personified.

"On the other hand, temporal expression as pleasurable sensations derived from the gratification of sensual appetites is only the base of mortal materialism. This miniscule form of orgasmically expressed infatuation is often confused with the more fully sacred Eros, Love expressed as the deepest passion for Life Itself, and extended to others as the divine expression of compassion. When beings finally learn to express themselves in Lovemaking with the fullness of Eros, then true Oneness, the ecstasy of Godliness, rules supreme. This divine spilling of one Being into another by completely letting go of resistance and control is a giving of Oneself to another in the fullness of Divinity. This is innocence that is to be savored, replacing belabored infatuation.

"The more common day to day expression of Loving that we're talking about here demonstrates the disposition to do good, having good will; kindness; charity; a Loving of mankind, accompanied with a passion for promoting their happiness. One delights in the happiness of another. Loving manifests as affectionate, passionate, engaged, zealous friendship, which emanates from respect for worth and amiable qualities of another; it is a noble attachment to another by virtue of confidence and integrity in relationship. It demonstrates Universal good will toward all. It is the noblest passion that animates one in the character of a good citizen. It comes to the fore in being polite, discrete, and courteous. Loving responds to others out of natural impulse, spontaneously, without reason, deliberation or instruction. Loving shows itself through a disposition to be merciful, a heart that is tender, moved by the distresses, sufferings, wants and infirmities of others. It represents a high value, great regard, favorable opinion, founded on one's own or another's worth; expressing reverence toward someone, as would God.

"Now, I ask you once again, how many of you regularly express these characteristics attributed to loving-kindness?" To no surprise, all hands enthusiastically rise in unison. "Ah, yes," Christo reinforces. "This is how each of us gives glory to God—and to the Godliness in each of us. All of us, each in our own unique way, demonstrate this to a high degree. Learn now to see these demonstrations as sacred, for each of us is sacred in our Being when we are doing so.

"Loving as previously described seems almost incomprehensible. Yet, if we take the occasion to deliberate how these aspects or characteristics of Loving have found their way into our very own lives, we would soon realize that, indeed, these are the ways we are loved by God, both directly and through others. As we become more and more aware that God exhibits Loving through each of us, lends us to one another this way, we can come to respect the dignity of Loving for all, in all. Perhaps even more important, merely because we rarely ever think of ourselves in such lofty terms, it would serve us well to visit this same list and ascertain when and where and how we have demonstrated these characteristics, these same aspects of Loving. By doing so our capacity to understand our real nature can be indelibly etched on the lining of our heart. The main point here is to come to know that God demonstrates Loving in all these ways and more. Because we are God's Idea or Image, Reflection and Likeness, just as Jesus was, we, too, can and do demonstrate Loving in all these ways, and more. Through grace, such demonstrations affirm Jesus' admonition that Loving is the way and the Life, and God and we are full partners in it. This sacred partnership is the real meaning of incarnation.

"All too often in today's society we see Love demonstrated as little more than shallow materialism. In this context, the real idea of love becomes quite trite: self-serving courtship and superficial, safe expressions of amorousness; lewdness; objectivism; self-absorption; egocentrism; vanity; infatuation; idolatry all. All of this can be transformed to the degree that we allow the Higher Self or Love to be demonstrated through our Being. Triteness gives way to Sacredness. Eros rules in its place. Self-serving infatuation transforms into eternal Courtship. So, as God is Loving in all these sacred ways, we also are Loving in all these sacred ways. As God's Idea and Likeness, we exhibit each of the correlative characteristics; and the trite and bastardized errors of thought, lived as illusory love, disappear from our demonstration. Finally we succumb to being Lovers of the Highest Order. We do nothing but engage and create and express Lovingly with the Divine all day, every day, throughout eternity. We, in the likeness of God, are the Truth of Loving personified.

"In order to lock in these understandings, I have found it helpful if when I do an inventory of how I am behaving I can also recreate the feelings I felt when behaving in a certain way. It is also helpful to become aware of feelings when interacting with, or even creating thoughts about, certain others. We all know when what we have just said or done "just feels right," when it clearly makes you feel good, glowing inside your heart. These are the feelings we want to recreate time and time again. This is not to say we deny those dark feelings we feel when we have an unkind thought, or have manifested a hateful act upon another. Not at all. Such dark thoughts, often repressed, are our informants. They tell us with indelible clarity that we are behaving in an unloving manner. They are the beacons that point the way for us to make the very next decision: how can I change what I have just thought or done to something Loving in its place? This is Loving creativity personified, expressed in the authenticity of our intimacy with God within.

"Just recently a new acquaintance asked what I did for a living. As usual, I responded: 'I make Love all day.' After an ever so brief pause, she said, 'Ah, with the Divine no less.' In all the times I have answered that question in this fashion, this was the very first person that got the Truth of the answer right on, at least out loud. So much are we engaged in the material world rather than the spiritual. Of course, my response is geared to awaken others to that very situation for themselves.

"This is a bit heavy and a lot to absorb, although I am confident each of you is up to the task, even though you may not feel so at the moment. What we all need now is some grounding, so I am going to suggest that we take an hour break to do just that. It will be helpful for you to take several deep breaths, for we often forget to breathe when we are engaged in an activity that fully absorbs us. On a warm, sunny day like today, it might also be a good idea to take off your shoes and socks and walk around the grounds barefoot; and don't be bashful about squishing the grass between your toes. This is a marvelous way to reconnect with Mother nature, the Holy Ground upon which we all stand. Otherwise, you're liable to fly away from all the inspiration you have absorbed thus far. Taking in some healthy material nourishment is also a good way to get grounded, as is eating a small amount of pure, dark chocolate. Just ask within what it is that you need at this juncture and get out of your own way. The answer will be clear soon enough. See you in exactly an hour."

As Christo leaves the podium he feels exhilarated by the engagement in Loving connection with the participants. He feels the growing God-confidence in each of the participants; their energy is that strong in its expression. He wonders, however, if they could be stretched even further upon return, or whether he should just summarize for now and return for more at a later date. Just as he begins to wonder about all this, a knowing smile comes across his face, reflecting his assurance that his awe over the Truth of the matter would soon have an opportunity to be expressed. In full appreciation of his own need for grounding, he takes out a small bit of dark chocolate and savors it with rel-ish, stopping only to wash it through his system with a refreshing gulp of water now and then. With this, he sheds his jacket and folds it neatly into a pillow as he gently rolls onto the ground for a brief respite. He lets out a deep sigh as he closes his eyes, knowing that everything he needs to continue his presentation would be sharply focused when he awakes.

CHAPTER 4

Living the Miracles We Are

After a fashion Christo awakens with a smile broadcast far and wide, feeling both completely refreshed and fully aware of what he must now do. He gives himself a few moments to refocus and then proceeds to walk through the returning crowd so he can gauge their readiness for the next portion. It is clear that there is complete congruence between need and direction. Once again his reliance on his inner Authority affirms his trust in it. Those who are privileged to have Christo pass near them on the way to their seats feel a decided surge of energy pass through them, as though he and they have somehow linked hearts. Christo clearly feels the connection, which tells him that the participants should be completely vulnerable to the last of the Truths that would be coming their way that day.

As Christo approaches the podium, he feels the crowd bathed in the glow of inner understanding. Now is the time to show the practical aspects of Loving expression, starting with the real meaning of miracles, so everyone could see their proper place as the miracles personified. As usual, he begins: "Namaste, I lovingly acknowledge that you and God are One. There, I've said it as the Truth it is. Let this sink in until you know its Truth in the depths of your heart. Actually, you already know it's in your heart; you just need to reconnect with it, remember with it. This, too, will come with time, with proper curing." He pauses for a moment so his proclamation can settle in. "All right, then," Christo continues, "it seems to me that we had better begin to cement your understanding of what you really are by dealing with how that is expressed in everyday life. Let's begin with this.

"First, let's look at how you could possibly be involved in manifesting miracles. A scary topic, eh? Earlier, I could feel anxiety rise out there when I had the audacity to suggest that you indeed have a great deal to do with miracles. Please, trust me this one more time. At least be open to the possibility that this is so. This recap, I am convinced, will help you see miracles in yourselves, perhaps maybe even *as* yourselves.

"Throughout the Bible, stories of the miracles of Jesus abound: the changing of water to wine at the wedding feast at Cana; the healing of the blind man Bartimaeus; the raising of Lazarus from the dead; and the healing of the cripple alongside the pool of water. It is said that Jesus made the blind to see, the deaf to hear, the paralyzed and crippled to walk, and drove demons from the insane—miracle after miracle after miracle.

"If we hold these miracles as only literally true, their impact on our Spiritual development is greatly diminished. By holding Jesus to be the only miracle worker, we severely limit ourselves from 'doing even greater works than these,' as Jesus said we could and will. But first we need to define what we mean by miracles from a non-literal perspective. As a sort of review, instead of a physical impairment, might not blindness be those dark thoughts, or preconceptions on any given issue, or other ways of thinking that are self-limiting, attitudinally negative or narrow, judgmental or self-righteous? Any of these perspectives can blind us to Truth. They can keep us only at the surface of relationships with ourselves, God, others and things, and can render us blind to the ways of authentic Loving. Each is an infirmity of Spirit. Taken to the extreme each becomes a crutch upon which we lean to avoid our inner Truth. Each can cripple us, become the bed upon which we sleep, and drain our life-blood from us moment by painful moment.

"If we choose to experience events as negative, or to be humiliated or embarrassed or somehow demeaned, Life itself will also be negative to our way of thinking. If, on the other hand, we choose to know in our heart that we are Loving Essence, and manifest our lives and see others the same way, Spiritually, then we give the Loving experience to all Life sends us. Knowing that, the pure of heart see right past the 'negative' act of another, right into her or his heart, thus forming the image only of the Loving Essence the other actually Is. This perspective permits the perpetrator to be seen in her or his Divine innocence and thus to be freed from the need for forgiveness before any act is ever committed. To see in this fashion sheds new light on those shadows of our Soul that have kept us blinded to the ways of Loving. We suddenly have eyes with which to see—and do, in fact, really see, perhaps for the very first time since birth or early childhood. Our new way of seeing Life becomes Sacred. Life becomes Sacred for me when I remember to see others in their Essence rather than as the result of the domestication process that wounds us all. In the context of Essence, both the moment and the other person are Sacred, and nothing else matters. Is this not the real secret of *being* the miracles?

"What is meant by being crippled? Cannot a withered or otherwise deformed limb be a metaphor for an attitude of idleness, laziness, self-centeredness—or any character defect, for that matter? It is said that an idle mind breeds an idle body. A mind bent on Loving ways, on giving up oneself self-less-ly to another or to a just cause, quickens the heart and limbs to perform that which one must. Freedom becomes not the strength to do what one wants out of emotion or self-indulgence but rather the power to do what one must out of one's natural Loving nature. The Spirit moves or quickens us and we are free to act. Fully energized by our joy-filled heart, we cast our mental and emotional crutches aside and set about our business of Loving authentically. In the form of a new perspective, our withered limbs are provided the spark of life that mobilizes them to action. The crutches of self-pity and fear have been cast aside, and the cripple has been healed. The man keeping himself from the healing that can only come from immersing himself in the flow of enlightenment—the sacred river—can also make the choice to heal. As directed by Jesus, he can choose to pick up the mat upon which he has placed himself, the bed he has made for himself, and walk through the meaning of past hurts in order to be healed. Once again, by opening the door to God's grace, he is shown the way, the Truth for himself.

"What about the leper? Does the term leper not represent those that are disenfranchised by any measure of physical characteristic or personal behavior? What is it that disenfranchises the leper? For some, certainly the way a leper looks. It is frightening to see the looks of one whose skin in being eaten away. It is also frightening to think of the potential for contagion affiliated with this dreaded disease. My questions for those who separate are this: 'What is it that you think you will be infected by? What is it that is eating away at you?' Are these factors also not those that drive some to separate themselves merely because one's looks, or even behavior, are different from their own? Or that they are afraid that they might therefore be contaminated by them should they somehow become affiliated with them? Such factors create separation and only fortify the fear that generates the separation in the first place.

"Given the manner in which many are now treating gays and lesbians, it is easy to see that these same fears drive them to this end. The same is true about those who speak differently than we do, worship differently than we do, come from a different part of the world than where we reside. Is the leper not the gay man next door, the lesbian single parent down the street, the black family that resides in the middle of a block of whites, the Arab who asked your daughter for a date, and the Yankee who chooses to reside in the South? On and on it goes, using any means possible to justify our separation from one another, despite the fact that in our origin, and in our image and likeness, we are One in being. What must we remember when we are confronted with an elevated energy around such concerns? Every time we are troubled by something we see in someone else, it is a gift that is there to prompt us to go within in order to see what we have disowned in ourselves. Remember the earlier example in the story of Bartimaeus. How could anything be so simple to discern when coming from our most natural state of Loving Essence? How could anything be so simple to apply in order to eradicate, or at the very least ameliorate, the differences we find amongst ourselves? Indeed, it is not the color of my skin, the nature of my speech, my religious affiliation, or sexual preference that determines my worth. It is the condition of my heart, that built-in image of Truth that renders us worthy simply because, as a child of God, I Am. 'Looks are only skin deep.' says the leper. 'Reality goes to the heart of the matter.'

"Have we not all been paralyzed by our limited thinking on such issues? When I see myself as being incapable, threatened or intimidated in a situation, I tend to "freeze." Figuratively, I am paralyzed in my thinking and in my ability to move on any front. When I remember to breathe and go inside my fear of the situation, the fear invariably takes me to Loving on its other side. My inner sanity is restored and both my enthusiasm and ability to move forward with dispatch reappear.

"And death—what is death? Physically our bodies can age, wither away, suffer, and cease to function, unless, that is, we learn to think of them in Spiritual terms. Metaphorically, to be dead is to be unaware of the quickening of the Loving spirit; to be asleep in a Life teeming with opportunities for enthusiastic expression of Love's many renderings; to be numbed to the divine passion that inspires within. We are numbed—indeed deadened—by the constant bombardment of sounds and sights; interminable messages from all the vast array of media; the electronic proliferation that strikes us from every direction; false expectations; improper demands; smoking and drugs; abuse of all kinds; on and on and on. All too often, we succumb to these external forces and take on coping as our way of Life, instead of recognizing these intrusions on our serenity and going within to deal with them in the sanctity of our heart. It is there where we yoke with our Divine Peacemaker, the Christ, the Loving way, where we will find other ways to think about such matters. The Truth of immortality quickly shows its face.

"A challenge, it seems to me, is to be able to define and live serenity in a way that finds peace, not without these intrusions but within them, in spite of them. When I find myself struggling, just coping with life, I know I am out of synch with living what I truly am. When I take just a moment in the middle of confusion or a struggle to center myself, I see Life from an entirely different perspective and Heaven appears once again. This takes continuous practice, and like anything else, it is the re-membering with the need that starts practice on its way. It is the re-membrance with the need for Loving that returns us to Loving. Indeed, it is the desire for re-membrance that is the catalyst, the Truth, which sets us free.

"A spiritual director once said to me that our purpose in Life is to be fully awake and to live like one who Is. Unfortunately, there are many who inhabit our planet who live money, power, and control—the gods and idols of an external life—as their primary sources of satisfaction, affirmation, and validation. The kinds of messages we receive from such people and circumstances place demands and expectations upon us that fit a world primarily in a daze. The abuse inflicted upon us is seen by the perpetrators as their way of guiding us to success—their success—but in reality, to what could easily become our demise in their ability to numb, to deaden our Spirit.

"If we permit ourselves to be numbed or deadened by these conditions and their impact on our lives, something or someone must issue the alert, the alarm that we have gone awry. From my observation, Spirit, or the Christ, is that alarm, the alert that calls to us. At times Spirit nudges us ever so gently. At others, we are called quite abruptly, to show us that we need to pay more attention to our interior condition. If we open the doors of our hearts but a crack, Heaven's trumpets will blare for us to test the condition of our Soul, to begin or reinstate our healing journey. When we have heeded the call, just the right people and circumstances begin to appear as miracles in our lives, sending us further and further on our recovery, toward our re-membering with the life of Lovers. Love's ways indeed appear toward our doorstep, in the hands and hearts of caring humans. Whether we pay attention, God still lends us for each other that way. Divine presence, in combination with our human counterparts, re-establishes Life as the perpetual Garden of Re-membering.

"If we treat Life as a perennial garden of sorts, we can learn to take on the perspective that its sole—and Soul—purpose is for providing opportunities for remembering to return to the purest form of Loving we Are: to sow either Lovingly or not, and to reap the harvest of either. So no matter what shows up in the garden, even if it looks at the moment like a weed, it is for our benefit. No matter what shows up, it is for our growth. Its means are to bring us to the single end of Loving. Each event, each person, object, or circumstance, no matter what the appearance—birth, seeming death and everything in between—is for the single purpose of moving toward our ultimate goal, providing we choose to see it that way. All we need do is to ask: 'How will this best serve me in re-membering what I Am? How is this serving my Highest Good—and the Highest Good of the person with whom I am now communicating?' The answers to such queries will nourish this new way of seeing Spiritually. The events that used to disturb us become our friends, our tools for learning about ourselves, rather than as infringements upon self-inflicted boundaries. We can be cripples or we can be free from impairment. The working of miracles comes from our collaboration with God, who has turned us into the miracles themselves.

"What about the insane? If we are not dead to the world, many of us are rendered, at the very least, insane: living the illusions of this world rather than the Loving Reality that is our birthright. The idle mind, the ego-centered persistence of serving self, or insistence on playing the political games of life, can indeed become boggling, restless, paranoid, manipulating, objectifying devils of the mind. Such demons can manifest themselves as physical, psychic and/or spiritual acts of abuse or unkindness toward ourselves, others, and things—whatever we draw to or choose on our path. A change of 'mind focus,' not at all unlike attitude focus, does wonders to render one sane in an insane world. For a time it will be difficult to accept the real Truth rather than those more familiar illusions that life in such a materialistic world perpetrates. But as fear of living in this *REAL* reality is conquered, our once-warped focus finds solace in Truth for itself—and real sanity, our inner sanity, is restored. The Truth of our Loving Essence comes from our In(ner) Sanity, rendering us In-Sane, with upper-case letters serving to remind us of Its sacredness.

"We can also come to our understanding of the purity of Loving by the perception of that which does its best to keep us from Loving: fear. Fear, too, can have its power over us. It can render us so-called insane. Fear is the greatest of the demons. In all kinds of insidious ways fear keeps us from moving forward. Fear seduces us into staying in places and relationships that are no longer appropriate for us. Fear keeps us from telling the truth to both ourselves and to others. It blocks us from standing up to bullies and others who abuse us. It keeps us in jobs that have long since passed their usefulness. It keeps us from even the simplest decisions, for fear of being wrong—or right. Fear keeps us from acting in the simplicity of kindness, fearing we will be stepped on, abandoned, or rejected yet one more time. Prolonged, suppressed fear turns into anger, sometimes violence, then depression, sending us to our real or imagined bed in an escape from the decisions and changes we must face within ourselves. Eventually it can even coax us to end life in this body. Fear blinds us, cripples us, it makes us think we're going crazy. Fear deadens our Spirit. Fear is a killer. Relationally it keeps us from dealing justly with ourselves and with others.

"If we examine life closely, we will realize that justice in Life can be dealt with in two basic ways: out of fear or out of our more natural Loving character. If we administer justice out of fear we do so with condemnation, punishment, revenge, bondage, and death—crippling perspectives to be sure. On the other hand, when justice is administered out of an attitude of Loving, we act out of forgiveness, freedom and growth. Fear is judgmental error, and it degenerates our very being. Love forgives and regenerates us in every way. Judgment or Love: to simply cope or to Be. When we have learned that we are Loving Essence and demonstrate our most exacting character or nature with every one and thing, we can at last know that we are One. It is in this Oneness that we come at last to fulfill the Sacredness of human dignity. Fear, the cleverest and most powerful weapon of mortal mind, keeps us from our Truth, from living authentically and genuinely as the True Self we Are, from being authentically Loving.

"If we can just remember that we are the Essence, Loving, and not a who, or roles we play, then the fear of not meeting someone else's expectations for who we are, or are to become, will soon leave us. The same is true for the fear of not gaining another's approval unless we behave in a way suitable to them. This, too, is conforming to who they want us to be, rather than to what we really, authentically, are. When we dispose of our addiction to external validation we are rendered the complete Being we already are. Expressions of genuine Loving for us are attained, and Life changes for the better quite dramatically.

"Yes, fear is the greatest of cripplers. When we let our fear-filled thoughts instead of our fearless hearts run our lives we soon see that it is fear that contracts our arteries, shunts our circulation, expresses lethargy through our energy, dulls our senses, casts a cloud of depression on our view of life, and distorts the Truth we are to follow. In actuality, fear is a distorted use of our faith. Instead of placing our entire faith in the Truth of God within, by living in fear we are placing our faith in thinking negatively about the potential in current conditions and circumstances. Living in fear places our faith in the worst possible potential for us: the fear of the abusive, deleterious past once again visiting itself upon us. Such misplaced faith, when harbored firmly in our thoughts, can only produce what its demonstration fears. As we are learning, God's job is to create, and God makes no distinction as to what God creates. God only follows what we say our faith is placed in, what we are committed to, what our convictions are. Based on whatever we declare in this way, it will be created through us. This is God's law of creation, and it will be followed to completion—unless some countervailing thought replaces it. So it all boils down to choice once again. In what do we place our faith: love or fear? Whichever it is, it will be our Heaven or Hell, and it is we who will have placed ourselves there by the way we invest our thinking, our faith.

"Fear's close relative, doubt, cleverly disguises itself as the simple questions that seem only to want us to be sure if the decision we have made is *really* right for us. Doubt is tied to that part of us that fears change, success, prosperity, approval and the many other gifts of Universal Love just waiting for our acknowledgment and acceptance. Doubt is the seed that sprouts into layers of dark clouds that keep the Light of our Spirit from shining on the Truth for us. Faith means moving forward without doubt. The healing idea is that faith is moving forward in spite of doubt.

"From time to time I have collaborated with spiritual companions, permeated by regular assistance of the Christ Spirit, in exercising the fail-safe process I took you through earlier today. I'm sure you recall the one that takes the plaguing thoughts that occur in our troubled, fear-filled, mortal minds directly to our fearless hearts. Just to reinforce the power of that process, whenever we harmoniously engage potentially troubling thoughts with intentions only of giving authentic Loving to one another, as a ritual we place our left hand on our heart and our right hand over their left hand that is also placed on their heart. This symbolizes the necessity of transferring, displacing if you will, the fear-filled thoughts to the Light of our fearless Hearts. We strip the fear-filled thoughts from the other by receiving them through our left hand, the symbol for receiving, and purify them in our own hearts, as bridges to assist in the healing thereof. We then send out the healing entity, Loving-kindness, the healed thought, back to the other's heart through our right hand, the symbol for giving. With regular practice we come to quickly envision completely different responses to Life: Loving responses, rather than ones filled with fear and all the pain that the ultimate fear of separation engenders. This Loving assistance to one another is similar to the previously mentioned exercise of drinking from the spigot of another's unfettered Loving Essence. Both work to the same ends. In fact the process and the end, Lovingly healing the pain of separation—or at least the fear of it—become one and the same. Oneness with Loving, both to ourselves and to others, is thus restored. Whether we replace fear-filled thoughts with some from another or simply within ourselves, we can be assured that the strength and clarity of our conviction will carry the day. Conviction erases the negative from within, from the pattern that would normally create that very thing we feared without. We create instead the blossom of our greatest good.

"When we fail to clear such fear-filled thoughts and all their relatives, they act as boulders that fill our situational knapsack. Each, when manifested in anything other than the peace that Loving brings to Life, takes on the character of a boulder that weighs us down. Fear does it; doubt does it; angst does it; and anger does it. The list is endless, really. Each time we take on an emotional boulder instead of facing it and then casting it aside as the illusion it is, it is tantamount to loading it in our knapsack, until one day we find ourselves totally weighed down with our situational litter. Eventually we buckle from the weight of all the tension, instead of making our yoke light by giving it to God as an act of Loving discernment along the way. Indeed, our shoulders become stooped from carrying the burdensome worries and petty declarations or claims of the nether world, errors all. When we feel ourselves laden with the problems of this world, we need but re-member with our commitment to join Loving in prayer, to fast from the errors in our thinking, and listen to Loving entreaties within, as admonished by Jesus to do. Regularly emptying our situational knapsack will raise to consciousness the need to deal with Life Lovingly as it appears.

"Fast and pray. Does this mean that we are to eat less, so that we can have a clearer, cleaner body, one relatively unencumbered by fatty tissue and toxic substances so that we can communicate more clearly with God? Not really, at least not in the spiritual world does it have this meaning. To fast, as conveyed by the Christ, the spiritual guide to our Inner Truth, means to get away from those negative or toxic thoughts that weigh us down, that take us to the depths of sadness and despair. It means that every time some negative thought or the appearance of difficulty or problematic circumstance bothers us, we are to replace it with the peace that only Loving thoughts toward another and ourselves can bring.

"With regard to prayer, for now it is good enough to understand that prayer does not mean to tell God what we want, or what our apparent difficulty is.

God is the God of All, is Omniscient and Omnipotent, and knows what is troubling us before we bring it to prayer. Therefore, the prayer we speak of here means merely to take the prayer we are into the silence of our inner Being, and ask God to speak; that God's servants, both you and I, are listening. The task is then to listen as you've never listened before. The more and more this is practiced, the better you will 'hear' Loving admonitions, Loving guidance. It will come in the form of the silent words in the stillness of being, as a feeling of relief or peace, as helpful words in a book or from a friend, or as nothing at all. It doesn't really matter how God speaks to us. What does matter is that when God does, we are hearing it, and being obedient to the Word for us, the only real Word for us: the Loving Word of Truth.

"Actually, even if we fail to hear and obey, the simple act of fasting, leaving the negative behind and opening up our temple for Loving to inhabit it, is an act of enormous faith, an act that shifts our thoughts from negative to positive, from heavy to Light. Heaven in earth appears in all her brightness, in all her peace, and in the joy of relief at being in the Presence of the Almighty. 'When thou prayest, enter into thy closet, and, when thou hast shut thy door, pray to the Father which is in secret; and thy Father, which seeth in secret, shall reward thee openly.' So Jesus spoke: Spiritually, metaphorically. In the closet of loving presence sit and listen with all you're worth, opening your heart to the gifts of grace, presents all.

"On the other hand, when we fail to commune with God to eliminate these negative beings or thoughts, these errors in appearance, eventually it is our body that becomes blind. It is our body that becomes crippled. It is our body that becomes insane, our body that becomes deadened. Is this necessarily so? Not really. Spiritually, we are blind, are crippled, insane, and we are dead only to the degree we permit our errant thoughts and beliefs to let us think it is so. Awake is the Soul that breathes Life into the dead. Awake is the Soul that inspires, energizes another to action. Awake is the Soul that provides a fresh perspective to one blinded by hurt, self-pity or judgmental attitude. And awake is the Soul that commands immortal Mind, and not puny mortal mind, to serve its Truth. In this Truth, we become One, as Loving partners. We are healed of sin, sickness and death as we know it, for there is only one real Cause, God. Therefore there is only one real Effect, the reflection of God in man as Loving and thus Lovable. Therefore, each of us is Perfect man, Immortal man, and Infinite man—the Miracle each of us is, and always will be. All else is error.

"Last, for now at least, let us understand that we have been seduced into thinking that we must tithe at least 10% of all we earn to the place of worship to which we belong. Indeed, there are stories that give every evidence that are those who do end up with much more in return, perhaps not even monetarily, but in the spiritual richness life so abundantly provides. Intention is the spiritual law that governs such matters. Taken as a concept this seems to work on the outside very well, but remember once again that the outside is only a mirror for what's happening in our spiritual life, whether we are coming from spiritual poverty or wealth. Just think for a moment, though, what might happen if we converted the idea of tithing to one that said that we give *all* of what we *are*, rather than a mere fraction of what we *have*, to God.

"Is this not what was meant when Jesus said to love God with all your mind, all your soul and all your strength? Is this not what is meant by always finding the God within, instead of fracturing our consciousness by sometimes going within and sometimes without for Truth, as though it could actually be found 'out there?' By giving all we *are* to God, that is, committing to the process of the interior life always, we are mending our house, our consciousness, that is divided against God. The results are so far richer than when we cast even 10% without, for we are afforded all the riches available in the universe of Truth just as we need them, moment by moment. How much greater can God's Sufficiency be? We can be witness to this sacred Sufficiency simply by changing our perspective on the meaning of tithing to correspond with the consciousness of loving creation: to being fully committed collaborators with God in creating lovingly for the benefit of all.

"Now that we have seen a variety of ways in which we can view ourselves as healers, as the miracles waiting to happen, just as Jesus was, let us make an important tie to a primary way in which we are akin to God(liness), in whose likeness we are increasingly finding ourselves. I have a sense that you all are getting closer and closer to the inner reality of Truth for yourselves. This last way to consider deals with our likeness as creators, emulating the Divine Creator.

"As it has been said earlier, we are God's idea expressed, uniquely as each of us is. This is the model for the universe of ideas. Ideas are parented or not, by choice—our choice. We often cancel out ideas as being too impractical, foolish, and selfish—you get the picture. More often than not, however, if we just deferred judgment on ideas and played them out into word pictures, they would gather more and more energy and we would find that indeed the idea is most worthy, more often than not in ways we would never have dreamt possible. As a matter of fact, when we do refrain from judgment on ideas that come brilliantly from within, whether we think that is so at the moment or not, we often find that all we need to do is listen, obey, and create from them. In this fashion we don't even need to weigh one or the other as good or bad. Judgment is in fact rendered nonessential to the creative act in its earliest stages.

"Perhaps I'm a bit ahead of myself here. Permit me to regroup and return to one of the major premises that serves as a foundation for our Spiritual life. That is, that God, as much as we can understand God, has demonstrated certain characteristics contained in the various descriptors for God, primarily Loving. Now I'd like to take you to one more descriptor that has been left until it has become more and more obvious that it is the guiding force for all the others. Said another way, there is a *process* through which all the others are made manifest and that is through the power of creation. Creation puts action into the expressions of Truth and Love and divine order. Creation puts the "ing" on the Word, turning Love into the formidable expression of Lov*ing*; turning Truth into Truthing, even though the latter would not be linguistically acceptable except as a convolution for a desired purpose. The fact of the matter is that many of our nouns can serve us more wholesomely as verbs and one would do well to consider this as an important framework from which to manifest a more wholesome, Loving, Creating life.

"Let's step back for a moment and see what our old friend Webster has to say on the topic of creation. Let there be no confusion as a result. Although God is the First Cause, Deity, and Maker, we have been caused to be in the image and likeness of God. What we can read in any holy scripture confirms this Truth. As the image and likeness of God, by exercising inspiration and intuition we, too, create, cause things to come to life, parent our brainchildren into the world. We formulate, design, develop, conceive, author, bear, and yes, even hatch ideas into reality. We imagine, express, manifest, apprehend, conceptualize, formulate, dream, deliberate, fancy, realize, muse, envision. We even forge, introduce, initiate, ascend, induce and deduce. How many of you express creation in any of these ways?"

As expected, the unanimous declaration voiced by all lights the entire arena in the understanding of this truth. "Finally," Christo thinks, "they're getting it!" Then he continues aloud: "*YES*, we do *all* of these—even *more* than these do we do. Creation can be thought of as our second nature, purely Loving being the first. The Truth is that lovingly creating is our more holistic nature for this time in creation's history. In this way Loving and Creating become One.

"It is abundantly clear that creation comes as a powerful process. It begins with an idea divinely inspired or thought intuited, both from the seat of the

Christ or Holy Spirit within. Ideas have a power all their own. Keeping them in the forefront of our thinking eventually takes them, often in a somewhat revised image, into words. We speak about our new idea. We write about them to others, or we begin to shape them into some kind of plan or design for life. Ideas in word form take on an even more powerful energy than an idea simply racing around in our heads. The energy of ideas spoken, either through the power of sound or imprinted word, is profound in its impact. It is when we decide to take the next step that the power is again multiplied, this time exponentially. Ideas transformed into word, then into action, propel the Loving energy forward with the power to transcend in the form of spirit manifested.

"Several years ago this came to me in a very special prayer method I was then using. I use it often still for its power to inform with absolute clarity. It doesn't tell me what I want to know, for the sheer sake of knowing. No, it tells me the Truth about what I need to know Spiritually at a particular point in time. At this particular moment my soul was nudging me on the creative bent. Here's what showed up:

> 'Your imagination is profound it its nature and impact. Let it run wild and let all that comes flow unimpeded by judgment. Merely go with the flow and have fun with it, no matter how crazy it may seem at first. This is Life filled with joy and it seems not to be work at all. Demonstrate your imagination and do not let thoughts otherwise enter. They have no place in your universe of ideas. Anything contrary to the imaginative essence of being is but a figment of fear and has no place. Your imagination's children are born of inspiration, not by ego-driven fear of any kind. Be inspired today and always, living joy always.

> Write down your ideas as they appear to you and follow them down the road of demonstration. This illustrates My image as creator as none other can. Create, create, create, leaving no stone unturned. Inspiration would not be coming to you if it were not to be demonstrated through you. Do take it all and live it all now. There is no need to filter what inspiration brings at any time, for any reason. Inspiration is purely divine and will be so in demonstration. Live on in joy, filled fully with joy now, My beloved.

> Genius is inspiration demonstrated, and imagination acknowledged, accepted, fertilized and grown into the material. This is the perfect image of the God of Creation, Me, so be fully as Me now and always.'

"Well, there it is. How much clearer does it need to be? *Can* it be? Unfortunately words can usually muck it up, make it sound more complex than it really is. We can think about this process as the power of Mind, Body and Spirit; we can think about it as the power of the Father, Son and Holy Spirit; or the power of consciousness, sub-consciousness and super-consciousness. On and on it goes, depending on the particular vocabulary one is accustomed to, is comfortable with. Like calling divine Authority 'God,' the descriptors matter not. The only thing that does matter is that the process is one we use daily, mostly without noticing that we are doing so. It is part of our nature to Lovingly express Spirit into matter. The purpose of our conversation today is to both acknowledge this Truth and to highlight the necessity of bringing the process into full consciousness. Once consciousness takes hold, we can collaborate in creating Lovingly for the good of our planet—all of it. This form is that which emanates as collective empowerment and lifts all to the ways of Loving genuinely expressed. Indeed, it is time that our collective consciousness be focused on deliberate demonstration of Loving acts."

Christo sees that the crowd is focused on this topic of creation and his inner Authority confirms the necessity to strike while the iron is hot: "It is said that the mind can endure only what the seat can absorb, and I don't see you squirming yet, so I'll go yet another mile on this one with you." His good judgment is quickly affirmed by the approving smiles he sees emanating from the gathering. "You're such attentive participants, so I think you'll benefit greatly from another slant on creation, particularly because many of the sayings attributed to Jesus will now come into play more predominantly. This will provide yet another opportunity for gaining meaning from the metaphorical as it informs the metaphysical."

"In Matthew, 5:45-46, for example, we find, '...for he causes his sun to rise on the bad as well as the good, and sends down rain to fall on the upright and the wicked alike.' In its context of loving one and all alike, the normal application of this Scriptural reference could well apply to exactly that in our material life. If God can love one and all alike, no matter whether they are good or bad in character, how can we do less? We must remember, however, that such references are to the metaphysical, not only to the physical world. In the metaphysical realm, the realm of thought, to what is this expression referring? For one thing, let's place it in the context of God's own law of creation. As I have said elsewhere, God's most important job is one of loving creation, out of God's promise to us. Because creation is one of God's laws, it must apply across the board. So if we are harboring thoughts about a particular thing we desire, and those thoughts are a form of thinking uncontaminated by negativity such as fear, doubt, or angst, then God will rain the resources of the Universe upon that desire, that expression of thought. 'It is your father's good pleasure to give you the Kingdom of Heaven,' after all. You can be sure that it will be given, but not supplied by anything we demand. We must remember that God's grace is our sufficiency.

"However, it we are harboring some form of fear or doubt, one that casts a pall of lack upon our thinking, let us say from our childhood memories, then what we fear, that is, lack, will be what is created. God has no choice in the matter, for God's law says only that God will create that to which we commit our convictions, our faith, whatever our predominant thought is. In the latter case, even though we committed our faith to a particular thought, another one less desirous, to be sure, ruled the day. God, without judgment, only spread its creative energy through the prevailing thought no matter what valence was placed on it.

"Indeed, God shines and rains creation, all of the Universe's holdings, upon that thought which we most strongly send out to God. If it is fear we send, it is fear we will receive. If the predominant thought is Loving, it is Loving we will receive. All we need to remember is that our convictions must be pure, hopefully purely for good. If we get something other than that which we thought was clear and pure, it is only because our thinking was not clear and pure. No big deal. Actually this, too, is a gift, for it tells us that we had better go back and investigate what it was that was incorrectly coloring our thinking to such a large measure. Then we can have another crack at it and see what that brings. Thus, even though we may temporarily think something is bad, we can come to understand that bad cannot visit any of us who sees and is convinced of nothing but good. Again, it's a matter of choice, of how we want to see life in and around us. Metaphysical treatments are this simple, for all they deal with is the manner is which we engage our thinking. This is the way we come to see that Life is the gift It is, no matter how it may seem in the moment. It all heads us in the direction of good, if we simply apply the appropriate thinking to bring good about.

"This perhaps runs against those who fear mistakes, but it is this Truth that must prevail: if we are aware and awake, an error is only that which leads us to newly formed thought and related demonstration. In this way we are falling into agreement with the way Jesus admonished us to live, understanding that no one need suffer more than once for an error expressed. As we came to understand in the parable of the man along the water, we need only to 'take up our bed and walk; thy sins are forgiven thee. Go and sin no more.' In the context of creation, and our responsibility in this sacred process, we are thus admonished to only acknowledge and understand our error, create a corrective thought, and then stop thinking about the error. This is called forgetting and forgiving. It's about repentance, moving forward in a new way. We don't need to be at all concerned about that error repeating itself unless we carry it around in our mind as a burden, gathering other erroneous energy around it until it manifests once again.

"In all of creation the conscious mind is the master, for whatever it focuses its energy on is what will be created. However, if one wishes to create, or to have created by God—a more truthful way of putting it—in a way that only good comes to be, then it would be wise for us to tap into the Truth of the heart for our direction and then command *that* from the seat of the conscious mind. After a fashion, this will become a regular pattern of creation. Such seeking of the heart becomes our new habit connected with creation, and nothing but good flows from and to us day and night. Such commitment destroys the house divided in a manner that recreates a collaborative arrangement instead, with the heart providing the Truth of any matter and the conscious thought serving only Truth in order to create good. In sum and substance, if mankind thinks predominantly evil, it is evil they will experience; if disease, disease it will be; if Loving, Loving-kindness will indeed reign.

"Creation also speaks to the Scriptural reference that, 'As ye sow, so shall ye reap.' This short, simple saying has been interpreted throughout the centuries to say that Jesus meant that any moral, ethical and lawful misdeeds would not go unpunished. It has been used by religion to inflict guilt on those who sow evil instead of good. It has been used by still others to create the realm of karma—where what we exercise as our moral and ethical behavior will show up again—one way or another. That has falsely come to mean that if we misbehave, or behave without being Loving towards someone, we sure as heck will have to pay for it, most likely sooner rather than later. 'Whatever bread we cast out onto the water is that which will flow back to us,' it is said. This is how those who invest their thinking on the material world think about this phrase. On the other hand, metaphysically, metaphorically speaking, 'As ye sow, so shall ye reap' speaks only to the spiritual law of cause and effect. A seed of thought sown in the garden of the mind shall reap only what it is: the blossom thereof, as it were. God only knows that it must reap the harvest of what the seed has sown, no matter what that is. Reality is created out of the seed of thought: this is creation personified. Whether the thought is moral or immoral, ethical or unethical, good or bad, is totally irrelevant to the product God must create. The seed planted, no matter in what form, must grow into the physical fact—this is the irrefutable law of God's creation process—unless the seed is uprooted and another planted in its place. The new seed will then grow to fruition instead.

"This may sound strange that God would allow us to create evil as well as good. Not really. If you allow yourself to think about creation in the context of freedom, the *absolute* freedom we are given to create *exactly* what we wish to create today and tomorrow and the next day, then you will come to see that God *must* allow us to create what can be billed as both good and evil. If that were not the case, we wouldn't have perfect, complete freedom. Again, God's laws are not made to apply in some instances and not in others. God's laws are uniformly applied or not at all. In this way of thinking success is the result of right thinking, not hard work or deservedness. If our thinking is wrong, or evil in nature, then it is not God that has punished us by creating something unto-ward. It is we who have punished ourselves. God only creates, not judges. Kah-lil Gibran portrays our part in creation so very clearly: 'Only then shall you know that the erect and the fallen are but one man standing in twilight between the night of his pygmy-self and the day of his God-self.' When consid-ered in the realm of creation, the expression, 'See no evil, hear no evil, speak no evil,' becomes a mighty powerful entreaty for us as well.

"Yet another Scriptural reference comes to bear on this process of creation: 'The sins of the father shall be visited on the son.' It is not, as usually portrayed, the immoral or unethical behavior of the father that is visited on his son. If we again but apply this expression to the metaphysical world of creation, as thought becoming reality, then it is the father's errors of thinking that are por-trayed out into the world, not only projected onto his son, but to all else that is touched by his creations. Whatever one projects onto the creative mind of the Universe will be attained, not only for sons and fathers, but for all else as well.

"Essentially then, we are responsible for only two things in the creation realm. The first is conception: from where do we get our thoughts? The second is our conviction, our placement of absolute faith. All the rest is up to God, and God can do only its work, just as our only work is found in conception and conviction. This keeps creation simple indeed. The only difficulty comes in remembering *our* part—and refraining from trying to do God's work instead. It was the Master Jesus who said, 'Come unto me, all ye who are bur-dened and heavily laden, and I will give you rest. For my yoke is easy, and my burden is light.' Can you now see the wisdom of this admonition? In case you are missing it, our part in creating everything in our life can be made simple, easy, and even light. All we need do is to simplify, simplify, simplify—by doing only what we legitimately can: conceive something for the good of the world, and unequivocally express conviction, our unfettered faith, in that and that alone. The rest is up to God. Hence, the Truth of the expression, 'Let go. Let God.' Do just those two things, do them well, and then give it all to God, earnestly, completely. Then, in God's own time, it will be done. Of that you can be sure. And so it is.

"By behaving and expressing faith this way we emulate Jesus perfectly when he said, 'It is not I who doeth the works, but the Father who dwelleth in me.' 'Who hath seen me, hath seen the Father.' 'I and My father are one.' He knew without equivocation that the ultimate responsibility of creation or healing, or any other demonstration, was not his. Jesus knew that all he had to do was keep pure his thought of creation and the purity of knowing the God in all beings. God did all the rest. He knew that it was not he who had to conjure up these thoughts, but that it was God that always created them in him, simply because he got out of God's way and let them come forth. Jesus also knew that this came about simply by listening for the sacred whispers in the stillness of his heart and then bringing such Truths into his conscious thought. I think perhaps all of you get the metaphysical, the metaphorical, meaning of this now quite differently than you might have in the past. In this way, too, we are cast in the perfect reflection and image of God, and Jesus, all in One. We now know our part in the collaborative creation process. All we have to do is remember it and exercise it consciously, by first going to the Truth of our fearless heart. In this we attain faith in the consciousness of God and none other.

"It is no wonder then that we can some to see in our hearts that God and we are One. And that all that is is of God, for we—all of creation—are One in being. Indeed, the Kingdom of God is within and we are full partners in exercising the Kingdom on behalf of all. 'All things are possible to him who believes.' It is this kind of faith that places complete trust in the power of God. We come to trust just as completely that when we conceive with absolute conviction, our brainchild will be perfectly created and delivered into the material world. Let us have faith that we will routinely conceive and express faith in that which is for the greater good of all. How affirming then, become Jesus' words: 'Be of good cheer. I have overcome the world.' He overcame the material by faith in the world of good thinking, using Eternal Wisdom as his own, the consciousness of God made manifest through him. The good news is that we can express life in the very same way. As long as we believe unequivocally, the same will ensue. We, too, shall overcome the error of materialism by faith expressed in good alone. 'As you believe, so will it be done unto you.'

"One of the gifts of this process of creation is that as we become more and more conscious of this process and more deliberately apply it Lovingly, those old, shopworn, ideas that depict self-absorbed greed begin to leave us. Soon we will have made a wholesale conversion, transcending the old with the new, pouring new wine into new wineskins. Our natural prophetic nature will be fulfilled in only the most wholesome ways. The real importance of all this is that we are, like it or not, created in the image and likeness of God. When we realize this Truth we begin earnestly to function as what we really are, rather than as what we have allowed ourselves to think and believe we are.

"Here is what we are not. We are not sinners, some kind of depraved entity, separate from God and one another, and born of original sin. Can you imagine God creating something that is not, in God's definition at least, good or even perfect? The Bible says that God created all and called it good. Can you therefore imagine that God created us all as one imperfection after another and that we have been placed on earth to correct God's work? That we must correct all the blemishes, remove all the tarnish, before we get into some place called Heaven—and if we don't, we'll go to some place called Hell?

"Can you imagine that some time, thousands upon thousands of years after God created life on planet Earth, God decided that It had a faulty creation pattern that manifested only blemishes instead of perfection personified? And that, instead of requiring that we work hard at removing our sins and blemishes any longer, God sent an ambassador called Jesus to save us from all our imperfections by letting himself be crucified mercilessly in our stead? Is God really that inept, so merciless, and so lacking in compassion? Yet many of our religious doctrines and mythologies teach exactly these things. How could we, as aware and awake, perfect manifestations of God's creations, as God's image and likeness personified, be so naive or so easily led to believe this about our God—or even about ourselves and one another?

"Is it not rather obvious at this time in our understanding that such false teachings were constituted as a means of creating and maintaining a power structure geared to inflict control of one body over another? As a means of establishing a process where we must depend on others for our salvation rather than our own individual relationship with our True Loving Essence? A means by which we can shed our responsibility for creating our life moment by moment onto Jesus, who has paid for all our mistakes, our sins, leaving us unaccountable for our own actions and for how they might, and do, impact on others?

"Let me make this abundantly clear, just in case any of you have missed it. We, as God's creations, are perfect. We always have been and always will be. We are perfect in the sense that we do exactly what we were created to do: create continually throughout life. Indeed, we create perfectly, one way or the other. Good or bad, it is creation nevertheless: perfectly so. All we need to do is come to, actually return to, that understanding clearly and precisely. Then our behavior, manifestations, and demonstrations will take on a new light, the spirit of enlightenment. And then our ideas and thoughts about others and ourselves will change dramatically, for divinity of thought manifests as the divinity it is. Nothing can change that Truth from reality—except as we think otherwise. Remember, we make our own Heaven or Hell, and the nature of our thinking is the determining factor.

"You and I are not birthed in original sin. We are birthed as God's perfection personified. We regularly demonstrate the ways and ideas of Loving and Being and Creating. What could be more the Truth than creating Lovingly in the image and likeness of God? All the divine, sacred characteristics of God are equally ours to demonstrate. Equal, I say, are we with God, for we are equal in the characterization of our being. Equal are we in our ability to Lovingly create. Equal are we in our capacity to express compassionate Loving passionately. Equal are we in our capacity to transform old ways of thinking and believing into the realism of Truth from within. We come to understand this sense of egalitarianism more and more as we come to understand that such behavior and creation is our real nature, and that we don't have to work hard to achieve such results. All we need to do is to remember what we are and live True to that, asking in the depths of our being: 'What is it I can do to express the highest form of what I Am in this circumstance? And what is this so-called highest form?' It is Loving expressed, no matter what, as the Highest Good for all concerned.

"Let's face it, each thought we have is a creation: each sentence we utter; each image we create; every action we initiate; each touch we make with another; and every time we exercise that which is our very Being in Loving Creation. We cannot avoid our creational nature. The difficulty comes when we construct a duality by thinking that creating destruction is the opposite of lovingly creation. In reality, the image and likeness of Loving, of God, is all there is. When we finally accept our True image and likeness we will no longer be able to ignore, or avoid, our Loving nature. In fact, they are married, married in the highest formulation of Godly expression: Creation Lovingly manifested.

"Being Loving is Godlike, is the likeness of God. Is there a higher definition of God than this: pure Loving expressed? I think not. Yet we are that same definition, and the same cause has the same effect. Is this not equality in its truest form? Loving begets Loving, nothing but. We create as God creates, within the same foundation of divinity, from the same seat of Loving compassion, in the same passionate expression of Loving as inspired by God. We extend that same inspiration to others regularly when we let ourselves be simply what we are. We are the transformational bridge for one another, until we can transcend the old for the new by ourselves, within ourselves, where Loving truly resides.

"Our purpose then, at least in part, is to help reframe how we think and believe about Life and our relationship with God and one another. In so doing we continually redefine a spiritual mythology that works for us and, hopefully, will benefit all with whom we come into contact. As long as we walk in our Truth, how could this be wrong for others? It really is none of their business to make that judgment. By going within we help reframe the concept of separateness and all the pain that emanates from separation into the Truth of Oneness, and of all the gifts of peace and joy that emanate from Oneness. When we form a bridge upon which others may traverse from where they are to where their God within directs them, we do so only until they can reframe Life for themselves. When they can do that, then they, too, are ready to lead yet others in an endless stream of transformative thought and action, transcending the mountains of erroneous beliefs and resulting pain and living the peace and joy that Life itself already is. This is God personified, and how we act in the image and likeness of the God that is called Loving Creator."

Christo pauses to catch his breath and to assess the character of his audience at the moment. He quickly checks within for guidance and decides to go just one step further at this juncture: "Folks, I want to take just a few minutes before our next break to tell you about marriage, what marriage is really about. For our purposes here today, you can consider marriage as the path upon which we must travel if we are to have authentic enthusiasm for the loving way. 'You mean we must be married if we are to have a fully loving life?' you ask. Well, yes, but not in the usual meaning of marriage.

"Over the years, marriage has taken on the demands and burdens of civil and/or religious law. In this day and age, marriage is taken literally to mean man married to woman—forevermore. When Jesus spoke about himself in the context of the bride-bridegroom couplet, surely he was not speaking about any of us being literally married to him. There must be a hidden meaning in his words about marriage. Perhaps this is to be found in the words' spiritual intention. My, oh my, can you imagine that?" Christo teases.

"In Biblical Scripture the word 'marriage' is used to represent the union of God with his people or of Christ with his church, the congregation of all who commit to a life of Loving-kindness. When one considers marriage, then, one must place his or her consciousness, energy, and commitment in the direction of being united first and foremost with God. In the spiritual sense, when you are married to God, truly at One with your God within, there is no person or circumstance or condition that can diminish or destroy that marriage. 'What has been formed with God cannot be torn asunder.' Except...

"If marriage represents our union with God, or Loving, what is it that can then tear it apart? Only when one breaks that union, thinks and thus acts in ways contrary to, or in the absence of, the Loving Way. In a real sense, this is the adulteration spoken about that is the only thing that breaks a marriage. Scripture hasn't really said that the only way one can be divorced is if one or the other member of the partnership between man and woman has committed adultery. Spiritually, what it is saying is that the only way we can be separated from our union with God is when we adulterate ourselves to this sacred relationship that is Oneness. The same follows in our relationships with others, whether we are married according to civil or religious law or not. When we separate ourselves from our relationship with God, that is, our way of moving through life only by Loving, and by nothing contrary to Loving, we have adulterated ourselves to this way of thinking about relationship and God. Therefore, in that determination we are automatically separated or divorced from God, our only just relationship.

"Should you reach the point of being that which is not Loving, of acting contrary to your natural Loving nature, you will not only be separated from God, you will be separated from all beings and things with whom you practice that which is contrary to Loving. Loving doesn't actually have an opposite, like fear or hate. Life in which Loving is the most natural state of all is simply that. When one lives other than Lovingly, there is no name for it. It is simply not Loving, or unloving if you must have a word to categorize such action. You don't really need a word for this, however, for one either is thinking Lovingly, behaving Lovingly, or he or she is not, plain and simple. And all of us can tell the difference between the two.

"When we are not Loving, we are indifferent to it, and when in difference, we are devoid of the energy and commitment to fulfill what we really are, the Loving Way. Some fear to be Loving, for whatever reason, but whatever it is we fear the most, that is what our heart is beckoning us to do the most, for it is our eternal Truth beckoning us with all it's worth. The greater the fear, the greater is the notice that this is what is most important to you. The choice becomes whether or not to obey this Truth as it speaks to you.

"When we create this separation we must understand that God never does. It is only we who do so. This extends to our feeling nature, and we soon find ourselves feeling lonely, out to sea, adrift, lost, depressed, disconnected from all of the rest of life—and thus without purpose. This is because our only purpose is to Love, no matter what the circumstances. Of course this applies to ourselves first, for if we are not Loving to ourselves, nourishing the Soul within us first, by doing what is best for our highest good, we can be of little use in Loving another with integrity. We would be trying to do so out of depleted and diminished Soul.

"There is only one way to eliminate these feelings that come with separation: marry once again. I'm not speaking here of marrying physically to another in yet another civil or religious ceremony, although that, too, under the right circumstances, can help erase separation. What I am speaking to is re-membering with your natural state of Loving once again. Reconciliation is really that simple: merely re-membering with what you and all the rest of the universe are by that very nature: Loving.

"When in a relationship in which you or the other has stopped behaving Lovingly, meaning while committing adultery, you don't even have to behave Lovingly with that person to reinstate marriage. All it takes is for you to open your heart once again to Loving—even with the flowers in your garden, or your dog or the neighbor's cat—and Loving will once again flow like a mighty river, unbridled by the vagaries of life. In these ways you are remarried to Loving, to Godliness. If you think this is silly or even untrue, just try this one-day and see what happens, and how you suddenly feel.

"Whenever you feel separated from Loving, separated from God, the Ultimate manifestation of Loving Essence, reach out with a Loving heart to the person you feel alienated from, have committed adultery against, God or another, and watch carefully for the response. Even if the other is hardhearted, thus committing adultery her- or himself, the illusion of separation will disappear in an instant within you. This opening of your heart will open you to a flow of more Love than you can imagine, and you will not only behave Lovingly to more than those flowers or that person, but you will feel like you have fallen in Love with the world all over again. Indeed you will have, for you and God will be reunited as One.

"Remember that how you think about the world, how you see the world, is how the world is for you, and not the reverse. It is independent of how others respond to how you are viewing it. We do not need another to return our Love in order for us Love, or to see Life as filled with Loving gifts. We only need to be that ourselves. It's akin to those who want their cake and to eat it too. They miss the essential point about life: it is they who *are* the cake, and all of Life is contained in it.

"Some would say that committing to a life of being in love with Loving could reap a heap of trouble. To do so would be to obviate those buried treasures, those disowned parts of ourselves that, if hidden, would only come to show themselves in some perverted or exaggerated form instead of more naturally. Such a thesis misses the point entirely. To be in love with Loving means we learn to Love it all, hidden or not, both the light and the dark within us. If from the darkness emerges a figment that is not Loving in nature, we can simply embrace it for the message it Lovingly delivers. 'Here I am, don't forget me,' is all that is necessary for us to hear. We merely need to acknowledge this supposed demon within us and face it with a heart overflowing with compassionate understanding.

"By being in love with Loving we apply the Loving understanding necessary to unveil the supposed evil for what it is: an erroneous figment of our own creation. It is anything we have disowned about ourselves that casts a long enough shadow for us to acknowledge and Love to pieces, literally and figuratively. This is the ultimate in intimacy: that we are intimate with our inner voice, our Inner Authority, no matter what shows up. I stand on this and this alone. Upon this we can build intimacy in all facets of our lives, in relationship with all others and things. Marriage to spiritual intimacy, and not separation from it, is that which drives the world, but most of us have yet to learn this lesson. We listen to fear in its place. Knowing the Truth about intimacy, and living it moment by moment, is that which sets us free to live from our fearless heart—free from an irrational life harnessed to our fear-filled minds.

"Now, how about all the divorce statistics we hear so much about? In the United States, the divorce rate has hit well over 50%. Why is this? If you consider what I have previously said in this regard, you will come to the quick, and proper I might add, conclusion that the reason that the divorce rates have escalated is because of adultery. I don't mean the kind of adultery that sends one or the other of the spouses into the arms of another. That kind of adultery is only a symptom. I mean the kind of adultery that is the cause of the one separating from the other in the first place; separating oneself from another emotionally, psychically, spiritually, and physically. It all comes about because one or the other, or both, either passively or aggressively, has stopped his or her Loving ways, has forgotten that he or she is nothing but a Loving spiritual being. In reality there is nothing but Loving. It is only the creation of an errant thought pattern or belief that sends someone away from Loving, that closes one's heart and puts up resistance to behaving Lovingly. It is solely, and soulfully, up to that person to make the necessary adjustment in perspective in order to return to his or her more natural state of Loving.

"Scripture tells us that Loving is all there is, that God is Love and the only way to a Loving God is through behaving Lovingly, every moment of every day. How much simpler can life be? Science has shown through studies of human behavior that when one is Loving, his or her endorphins increase accordingly. Endorphins are what enrich your blood stream, giving fresh energy to every cell, thus making you feel and behave younger—even look younger. As a matter of fact the great fountain of youth stems from the endorphins released by being in love with Loving and thus Loving lavishly. The endorphins released by both the Lover and one being Loved actually reverse the detrimental effects of not being so, of being caught up in coping with the egocentricities one generates in life. Even those who are only on the periphery of such Lovingness, who only witness its energy, are uplifted by this same energy. They, too, begin to reverse their own tragic accumulations of either being in, or affected by, the adulteration that flows around them. Simply put, our internal chemistry corresponds to how we live, and our bodies in turn correspond in harmony with our chemistry, one way or the other. Loving is the feature that provides the balance.

"Sometimes expressing Loving compassionately could even mean that one releases another from their mutual bond to one another if the most Loving thing to do is to release that person to what is the higher good for him or her. If you and the other are to be together in the long run, she or he will return to you and renew those Loving ways. If not, there is nothing holding either of you back from Loving in any event, for it is always we who get to make the decision of whether to Love or not, even if it's Loving another enough to let her or him go on their journey without us. Our only purpose is to stay Loving, true to our nature, and thus living in our own integrity. If another chooses to manifest that differently or somewhere else, that is no skin off our nose. It is not a personal thing at all, and the leaving has no bearing on whether the one left behind is, or can be, Loving again. One simply chooses to Love or not.

"To think otherwise is to take ourselves way too seriously, and the actions of others way too personally. The actions of others toward us have nothing at all to do with us. They have only to do with their need to express themselves exactly as they do. If they are being judgmental toward you, for example, it is not because you are not good enough, but rather because they have a need to be judgmental, most probably about themselves. This is merely projected out on to you, who serves as the screen or mirror for them, so they can see this in themselves.

"When you take this line of Truth to relationships of all kinds, familial or not, it becomes quite clear that we are never really married to anyone or anything but Loving. We may flirt with other ways of manifesting our lives, but marriage is reserved for our relationship between God, that is, Loving, and ourselves. In a real sense it makes no difference who or what we're talking about. We are either married to Loving or we are not, and we behave whichever way we have chosen with everyone and everything else. This makes the topic of gay marriages, for example, a non-sequitur, a nonstarter, for the only thing that matters between us and another is that we are allowing the Holy Spirit, as Loving energy, our Loving nature, to be authentically expressed through us. That act has absolutely nothing to do with race, religion, cultural background, or gender preference. The marriage in any relationship is to Loving, to God and God's ways, and not an individual, even though our marriage to God exemplifies itself in every other relationship in which we engage.

"Because we are spiritual beings, we are subject to spiritual laws, and the only real spiritual law there is is to be in love with Loving, with all we are, mind, body and soul. When we are, our life is filled to overflowing with Loving-kindness in all forms. Either we follow this law, are faithful to it, or we are not. When we choose a path, any path other than Loving, we are no longer married to Loving, because we have just committed adultery to our bond of Loving, our bond with our Loving God, and the God within ourselves and all with whom we come in contact. The seemingly unbearable pain that comes from the choice of separation inflows instantly, completely, and without let up. It is not God that has inflicted this upon us. It is we who have inflicted it upon ourselves, out of our unbridled self-absorption and self-indulgence, our bond with ego that we have substituted for the bond with Loving. Once again, it's all a matter of choice. Do we abide in God, in Loving, or do we abide in fear and indifference to Love's ways? One thing is sure: the pain of separation we feel is notice to return home to our most natural state of Loving.

"Well, this is all fine and good," continues Christo, "but what real good can come of living this way? Of course, our relationships should improve: our life's purpose will be clear and regularly fulfilled; we will be free from the inner tensions caused by feelings of separation; and we will be Lovers of the highest order. Even so, how will such a dramatic shift in how we discern and live that Truth effect our lives as spiritual beings in physical bodies? We'll take one last break now, and when we return we'll face this intriguing topic together. You might want to treat yourselves to a little snack so you have the physical wherewithal to head down the homestretch with me. We'll reconvene in thirty minutes."

Christo pours himself some soothing tea and places it alongside a plate of fresh fruit and cheese. He gathers himself and periodically goes within for spiritual nourishment to complement his physical tastes. He seems completely satisfied with himself. For the most part he has gotten out of his own way, and has let God speak through him. Even when he hasn't, he muses, he has only shared with the crowd what God had previously graced his presence with, and so he feels comfortable having served the multitudes, as he knew he must.

His Followers come to give Christo their sense of what is happening elsewhere. The report is filled with comments about spiritual overload, with conversations unbridled by past beliefs and indoctrination. In short, the place is abuzz with excitement, despite the momentary mental weariness of the day's penetration by the Holy Spirit. Christo knows all too well that this last session would put it all into a solid perspective that would serve the participants well as they head back home to engage the rest of the world. He instinctively knows that he has to ground them with something they can use as a basis for their actions when they go out into the world again. It pleases him immensely to think of the potential impact so many people could have on those they would inspire with their new perspectives on life. Indeed, he is very pleased.

CHAPTER 5

Creating a New Spirituality; The Key to Coming Alive

Christo rises and strides toward the podium one last time. He walks ever so slowly, drinking in the loving energy he feels along the way. He feels powerfully refreshed. The crowd seems to sense this, having learned in this short span of time how to read loving essence. What they feel in turn is the soaring energy that Christo casts back out into the crowd, and each is touched to the core, genuinely nourished for the last portion of this gathering.

"Namaste. With heartfelt appreciation I gratefully acknowledge the loving God in each of you…the divinity you are." Once again Christo places his left hand over his sacred heart and extends his outstretched right palm toward the crowd, making sure he sends it in every direction. "Now, each of you, do exactly as I am doing: place your left hand over your heart, opening your heart just enough to let the best fruit of your divine wine press flow gently outward. Then extend your right palm out in front of you and send that long, sweet draught of loving spirit out across the arena. Let it just be for a few moments, and as it strikes you from others, drink it in until you are full to overflowing. Now, do this in memory of your time with God today, and know that it can be the same all day, every day."

He pauses for several minutes to let the fullness of loving expression permeate the crowd. The arena is aglow as if the lights had been turned on for a TV production of the NCAA final championship basketball game, but the sensuality of the glow is much deeper and richer and more golden than the harsh, artificial light that comes from those lights. You can feel the "hum" of loving energy permeating one and all. "Okay, now that you have felt the extent of Loving embrace that can enfold you, let's see how that can affect you on your daily rounds."

But before Christo can begin, he hears a man from the crowd cast back to him, "Namaste, Christo, Namaste." Then comes another, and another, and still another. All at once the crowd becomes still, and in the next instant a unanimous "NAMASTE, Christo!" soars forth to Christo, and he is filled with the knowing that their lives would never again be the same. Christo relishes this enormous display of respect for what he is and how he has let God speak through him. It speaks volumes.

He gathers himself and then humbly proceeds: "Thank you, my dear friends. It is obvious that you have allowed yourselves to be at One in a most profound way. I am confident that you will be casting God's Love out in ways that will enrich life for all you touch, in exactly the ways you have been touched. For, you see, you are now disciples of Christ, the healing energy that restores life where it once was missing, that makes the deaf hear, the blind see, and the halt and lame walk once again in the Loving grace of our one and only God. You are something else, you are!" Christo says in tones of Loving appreciation and gratitude.

Again, Christo pauses to let this sink in, so everyone could leave with the understanding that they would be the prayers that would answer the calls for help. He is convinced that they now know how to hear the call and to serve as each must. "All right, then, let's proceed. I have given many examples of how a change in mythological perspective can benefit humanity. There is another compelling example of how treating life Lovingly can change our lives and those we touch; not simply touch, but profoundly so. Some years ago I began looking closely at the various energies that affect my body. During a week long intensive dealing with chakras, those spinning pockets of energy that impact on various aspects of our behavior, I was awakened to understand some important bits of Truth about the relationship between energy and the ways we act out our inner life. All in all, it could be, and most often is, a very complex relationship. I want now to provide a brief overview of that relationship, exposing the simplicity of the sacred connection between energy and behavior demonstrated. It is one that will at least open the doors to consideration for those interested in living a life that more directly and completely corresponds to their inner Truth.

"Permit me to begin by sharing some pertinent information about the flow of life at its very basic level, dealing with water. Later on we will extend what is true with water to the idea that water is merely a symbol or metaphor for our emotions or energetic expression out into the world. Deeper and deeper it will penetrate, much like a spiral, until we gain at least a preliminary understanding of our heart energy and how it can and does empower us in our daily lives.

"It seems to me that these understandings, or at the very least something akin to them, are exactly what formed the basis for the healing attributed to Jesus. In short, Jesus clearly understood the impact of certain perspectives, ways of thinking, and attitudes on our natural state of being. I offer what follows as a means of taking to heart an understanding that will convince you of the healing power of reframing one's perspectives on life and its relation to Loving Creation.

"From various studies of water over the years, not the least of which is the compelling research by Masaru Emoto, summarized in his piece entitled *The Hidden Messages in Water* in which were studied the effects of various energies on frozen water crystals. We can gain an ever-growing understanding about the relationship of energy to substance by understanding the results of these studies. For example, we know that water is an unusually powerful solvent. Almost any element or chemical can be dissolved in water quite readily. So much so, for example, that the moment we place pristine spring water in a plastic bottle it begins to absorb the chemical nature of the plastic. Hence the readily discernible taste that emanates from the chemicals that comprise the plastic container. I suspect few of us have tasted really pure water, water that has flowed freely in the highest mountainous streams, filled with the cleansing nature of the oxygen that has penetrated it when flowing unimpeded, merrily on its way along the stream beds.

"Contrarily, we all are aware of how our pristine rivers and streams have been polluted—allowed to be polluted I should say—by various chemicals and other harmful wastes. We are also aware of the continuing debates about whether the addition of fluorine and chlorine to our drinking water is really good for our bodies. Of one thing we can be sure: whatever comes into the world's water highways is absorbed into the matrix of this simple water compound. When we take water into our system we engage each element contained in it with the fullness of each cell, each molecule, each space that makes up what we call our body. We can, of course, say the very same about each internal fluid, including our blood and various other originally helpful fluids, secretions, and the various other forms of water that assist us in living a healthy existence.

"When we think about our rivers being polluted and contaminated by chemical substances it doesn't take long before we can trace the potential effects on our bodies. Yet, knowing that, we permit such travesties perpetrated and perpetuated upon the planetary society not only to exist, but also to flourish, all under the guise of economic gain and security. By permitting these travesties to continue we are committing to a wholesale divestiture of our body and Soul's health. And it doesn't stop there. Whoops—I'm getting on my soapbox here. I offer my humble apologies.

"The research I'm sharing with you today has shown us that not only do chemicals pollute and debase our existence, but that human emotions and thoughts, music, even written words, vary in their impact on the condition of water. Just as cleanliness and pristine conditions, free from acid rainfall and other pollutants, produce contaminant-free water, pure and completely healthy, so do thoughts and emotions that are Loving and stress free. One way or another, such treatments influence the condition of water to correspond, or resonate with, either the positive or negative thought forms—music, likewise. Classical music, and that generally thought of as soft and healing New Age music, have been shown to enrich the quality of water, while heavy metal music severely deteriorates its quality. It has been further proven in research that these forms also either enrich or deteriorate plant life in similar fashion. One could easily draw the conclusion, and correctly so, that because plants, like humans, are also largely made up of water, that it is the water quality in all of life that is either positively or negatively modified by a wide range of reinforcing agents, with only a few being merely neutral in their effect.

"Further, when water is placed in containers and certain positive words like 'love,' 'trust,' and 'gratitude' are placed alongside or 'prayed into' the water, the water is changed dramatically for the better, made purer. On the other hand, when more negative words like 'hate,' or 'anger,' or 'ugly' are placed in water's proximity, it becomes murky and unhealthy. When one gives quality consideration to the impact of pollutants of any kind upon our water sources, whether it is chemicals or other toxins, words or music, emotions or thoughts, is it any wonder that we are suffering from a serious deterioration of one of our primary life support systems? Is it any wonder that by consuming increasing amounts of water into our system daily we are contaminating our bodies to greater and greater degrees? As we contaminate our bodies we leave less and less space for that precious commodity, oxygen, to enter our bodies and cleanse what needs cleansing. Hence the need for antioxidants, those products that are supposed to assist in cleansing our blood. Wouldn't it be a simpler way, and much less expensive, to eliminate contaminants from our streams and bodies on the front end? Imagine a system of preventive health care that would replace expensive means of eliminating only the symptoms of a corrupt existence. What an interesting idea," Christo declares with a glint in his eye and a broad smile across his face, obviously pleased with himself.

"Think, for example, how we are contaminating our blood stream, composed mostly of water, and how that contamination relates to the condition of our muscle tissue, and the tissue of those organs that balance and sustain our inner physical life. Consider the tissue that makes up our arteries and veins, and perhaps the most powerful organ of all, that which pumps life's resources through our bodies. Yes, we do have mechanisms and organs for continuing to cleanse our blood, but if those organs are also polluted by the likes of unwanted fats, sugars, and the effects of emotional stress, what then is the likelihood of such mechanisms doing their job as it was originally intended? In a word: nil.

"When we clog our arteries and veins and every cell of our body with contaminants of one kind or another, how do you suppose the energy that is to course through our bodies uninhibited can flow as it must if we are to be energetically healthy? We have at our disposal the natural flow of energy that moves in and through us, and which assists in the healthy development and operation of our entire being. We have at least two forms of such energy. Kundalini energy is that which flows along our spine to all the various energy centers of our body. Tumo is that energy which is often described as the 'fire in our belly.' Tumo displays as the inspiration and enthusiasm we have for life that fuels our will to not only live, but to thrive in our relational society, and to create divinely as is our purpose: to express the natural outflow of our immortal and infinite nature as creators. Tumo is tantamount to being our internal burning bush.

"When such energies flow unimpeded and in a balanced way, we then operate as the divine beings we are, as the reflections of the higher power, by whatever name, we are. We divinely create out of a loving space those things and ideas that imbue our planet with beauty and grace. On the other hand, when any form of pollutant impedes such energy, the energy begins to coagulate, form pockets or clusters of energy, trapped as it is, and thus the organ or tissue cannot do the job for which it is intended. Instead of supporting life, the plugged-up energy builds and forms as resistance to flow, creating sore, often painful, reminders that we are energetically out of balance. This is how acupuncture and acupressure help to resolve such blockages and related pain and bodily dysfunction: they release the energy to flow more naturally once again.

"However, unless and until one learns to move the energy using meditative or at least a higher conscious understanding of what one is feeling, and an awareness of its mental and emotional cause—the pollutant or coagulant—one will become dependent on the practitioner to clear one's energy. There are many ways of clearing up such energy blocks. Meditation, yoga, regular exercise, a healthy eating regimen, acupuncture and an overhaul of mental thoughts and emotional states work well in this regard. One would do well to remember that the various forms of external pollution internalized and the degree of the pollution of our energy systems run hand in hand. They need regular cleansing if we are to become and remain healthy. So consuming chemical remedies and antibiotics to supposedly eradicate disease actuates the exact opposite effect.

"As the time to summarize the importance of these concerns arrives, I am reminded of two favorite quotes, the first from St. Frances de Sales: 'The spirit cannot endure the body when overfed, but if underfed, the body cannot endure the spirit.' And the second is from Marion Woodman: 'The Spirit without body is ghost; the body without Spirit is corpse.'

"For just a moment let's consider water, or even our blood stream, as but a symbol or metaphor for our emotional state. In the more spiritual considerations of life, water can indeed represent the emotions. If certain substances contaminate water, not only chemicals and other pollutants like music, thought and emotional energies expressed, how about our emotions themselves? Our emotions are no more, or less, than how we choose to respond to life's situations and circumstances; how we think of them. We do have a choice of how to respond. If we build into our emotional vocabulary a primary set of negative phrases and words and related actions, then our emotional state will indeed be, at a minimum, cloudy, murky, perhaps leading to one which can be volatile in character. If we persist in using such a negative setting as the lenses though which we view life, life cannot appear to us as anything but those negative labels. We become the victim of all life perpetrates upon us, and our relationships, our communities, churches, workplaces—all of life—is painted in that cast of darkness. In turn, each of one's cells takes on the negative energy, causing stress on the natural state of its being, polluting it to the degree it will, until and unless one changes one's outlook, one's perspective on life. One thing we know for sure: how we see things inside is how they will appear on the outside. When we change the way we see things, the things we see will change. Our whole being is effected by the relative energy we feel: healthy or not, positive or negative, stressful or filled with peace and joy.

"Now, for a larger, perhaps an even more profound blockbuster: the human heart is a source of great electromagnetic energy that drives our human physical existence and powers our spiritual connection. It emits this energy in a circumference some twelve feet around our bodies. That's right, twelve feet! The human brain also emits a similar energy out from the body, but only to the degree of approximately two inches. Why this huge difference? Well, for one, the heart is energizing the entire body and spirit, while the brain supposedly only energizes a few of the body's necessary systems, including various forms of thinking: linear, rational, symbolic, and otherwise.

"However, perhaps now is the time to understand that the heart has a function much different than heretofore understood. The heart is the "divine mind" that connects us with the Greater Being, God, by whatever name. It is that through which our higher self demonstrates—through which our higher thoughts and emotions, as well as individual and collective divine consciousness—flows. It is that which inspires and continually brings us back to our central purpose: Lovingly Creating for the Higher Good of all. The brain, often confused with the mind, is a very powerful instrument to be sure, but its primary purpose is to assist in carrying out the divine master-function of the heart. In this regard, it is precisely like the ego's relationship with the heart; the ego and the brain have, as their purpose, being in service of the heart, and not the other way around, the latter being a notion received from the Renaissance and the Industrial Revolution that has set us back in our spiritual development. The predominant line of thinking became the proposition that intellect and linear, rational thought were the primary, if not the only, elements in determining mankind's welfare. Not so. It is intuition that is connected with divinity, the clearest and most Truthful element in determining our purpose and the path that must validate that purpose.

"The intellect, rational thought, serves the heart energy, serves intuition, and not the other way around. Intuition is the energy, the sacred Truth, in which we are most naturally grounded, and upon which we are founded. It is the higher Mind, our connection with the higher Being, God, housed and made operative by a heart hopefully cleansed of pollutants, both chemical or energetic.

"Just as emotions affect and effect our attitudes and various bodily functions—physical, mental and spiritual—they have impact on the condition of our heart, for it is composed of those very same kinds of cells as the rest of us. If our heart is impacted, we can take the next step in understanding and discern that if our heart energy is in any way contaminated, then that which it sends out to touch others is contaminated in similar fashion. Permit me to share a brief story to illustrate.

"Just over a decade ago now, I was participating in a month-long program at the Pecos Benedictine Monastery in Pecos, NM, one designed to prepare people to become charismatic spiritual directors. After lunch one beautiful sunny day, I decided to take a long walk in the mountains in order to gain some solitude after a rather intensive morning of spiritual intervention. Heading toward a bridge over the Pecos River (River of Life), I felt an 'inner tug' pulling me toward the near side of the bridge along the river. I followed that prompting and began a moderately paced, but nonetheless contemplative, sojourn. Almost immediately, I felt another 'inner tug' suggesting that I walk closer to the edge of the river, along the freshly fallen snow. As I did, the beauty of the surroundings washed over me and the river itself seemed to beckon the flow of the Holy Spirit that now began to fill me.

"Before I realized what was happening, I found myself navigating my way to a richly textured beach inhabited by thousands of stones of all sizes and descriptions. Why, I wondered, was I attracted to this spot? The response from within burst into understanding almost before the wonderment completed its query. The stones took on entirely new 'clothing,' appearing as human hearts that had turned to stone for one reason or another. I remain convinced that I could have named every stone on that beach, their identity was that clear to me. One had been blackened by the oppression of all life appeared to be; another pitted by the stings of an insensitive spouse; still another split by the massive strike of unrequited love; and yet another marbled by dedication to the fatty lifestyle of a materialistic society. All this seeped in as I pondered its meaning for me.

"As my Mind's eye wandered, one stone with a human-like figure worn into its surface seemed to beckon me. I cautiously bent over and picked it up. Close inspection revealed a figure praying with its hands folded neatly at the waist, its head turned almost cavalierly to one side. No matter how I tried to see it otherwise, that head stayed fixed in the sideward glance. Using active imagination I began a dialogue with the figure on the stone. I only needed to begin for the answer to appear. I asked simply why its head was turned to the side and the response was immediate and profound: 'I lived my life with indifference and my heart turned to stone.'

"Suddenly I turned my attention to the large boulder in the middle of the river, recognizing that it was not entirely in the metaphorical or symbolic river called Life. Just as quickly I realized that one is either in life or out of it. There is no real middle ground, no part way. My gaze then went to other stones totally immersed in the river and they appeared as more fleshy counterparts of the beached variety. Their interaction, indeed, their interdependence with other beings had produced the flesh that comes only out of devoted interdependence.

"The metaphor changed before my very eyes as I stepped with both feet into the stream, symbolically committing myself to living totally in union with all Life is. I had come to the realization that one is either in difference or in Love, and there is no in-between or halfway about it. Just as we are the journey that makes our Life, we are like the stream that contributes to the making of the ocean. Later in the day scripture from the Book of Revelation (3:15,16) affirmed the message: 'I know you well—you are neither hot nor cold; I wish you were one or the other! But since you are lukewarm, I will spit you out of my mouth.' And so life does.

"Imagine then the energy coming from a heart blackened by a seemingly oppressive spirit; or one pitted by the stings of an insensitive spouse; another, split by the massive strike of unrequited love; or one marbled by the lifestyle of materialism. We all have felt such energy strike us, even repel us, from across the room or at a family gathering. Contrast this with the energy we all have felt when a truly Loving, highly charismatic person enters a room or becomes a friend. We seem empowered by such a presence, for indeed we are. The strength of the higher resonance that emanates from one who permits the divine to flow through to all who can be lifted by it is mighty powerful. Such is the power of Love's energetic flow—or the dimuntion of Soul that comes from the lack thereof.

"I return to a more recent intensive retreat dealing with the chakras to make another point. One of our concluding activities was to connect through our root and crown chakras with the power of the cosmos. After just a short time in this meditative exercise I found myself in the midst of the thunderous silence of space we call the cosmos. It was profoundly powerful in its depth of character, and its clarity and purity. We were then asked to find that same space in our bodily cells, for most of what we, too, are composed of is made up of space, interspersed with protons, neutrons and electrons. Like a mighty zoom lens, my knowingness took me into the innards of that space. To my great surprise it was identical to the space observed in the cosmos.

"Subsequently I was led to fill the space throughout my cellular structure with Loving, healing energy, the color being lavender. By this time it was relatively easy to do so, and I felt a new, extraordinarily powerful energy course through my entire being. Then we were asked to open our eyes and to describe the tree that hung overhead. The light was so bright I couldn't open my eyes, except for the narrowest of squints. I unconsciously let out a painful cry, as if coming out from a darkened theater into the bright sunlight, only much more painful. 'I can't open my eyes. It's too painful from all the light.' 'No,' responded our leader, 'its too bright because of all the energy you placed in your cells, not from just the outside light itself.'

"With this declaration immediately came the absolute understanding that it was this space that could be pure—or contaminated by every form known to mankind. Indeed, to a large extent it already was contaminated by the energy of the collective consciousness. To the degree that it is, it is as much responsible for the energetic, physical, mental, and spiritual disarray that exists as that we contribute to it. To know that this sacred space is contaminated by the energy exerted by both individuals and the collective was indeed astounding. It left me with the additional understanding that I don't have to take on the entire responsibility for the energy that fills my thought processes and emotional space. As a matter of fact the impact of the energy exerted by the collective consciousness far outweighs that of any individual, and thus greatly influences how we view and experience life.

"Such understanding leads me to know that if I want to be free of all that has impinged on the clarity of the sacred space that infills us all, all I need to do is place myself meditatively in that space, and occupy it with divine Mind in order for it to be purified. As I practice this way of purification I can do so with the realization that after a certain degree of practice, such purity will take over with a life of its own and not permit alien energy to implant itself in the space that only the sacred can properly inhabit. Thus this is the necessary first step, perhaps the only step, that needs to be taken for purity of life to be reinstated and maintained. This, to me, is the purest form of prayer, collaboration with the divine, harmoniously imbibing in all real Life is and has to offer. But for those who not yet ready or able to make this leap there are other ways that seem to have resonance with the Truth of the matter.

"This leads us most naturally to ask how one can possibly cleanse all that must be cleansed in order to fulfill one's purpose with clarity and with the dignity that Loving Essence commands? First, one must understand that our *most* natural state, actually our *only* natural state, is that of divine Essence. In reality it is the only real substance there is and thus can and does fill all space. It is only we, with our so-called linear, rational minds, who pollute all which can be. We do so by placing rational thought and egocentrism at the fore, in place of intuitional Truth. Such a choice can only lead to games of force, that which breed elements such as forced competition, greed, and lust, instead of leading a life filled with the power of Truth and all Truth engenders: the natural flow of Godly Essence through and to all. The former leaves us feeling empty and with our purpose unfulfilled, much like an egg with no yoke. The latter produces a deep feeling of resonance, one which can guide us clearly and decisively throughout life.

"Resonance is the feeling called for and felt when Truth reigns. It is grace personified and amplified. We have felt the resonance with inner Truth when confronted with everything from a right decision, a new, wholesome relationship, and an image of beauty portrayed. Each is in resonance with the divine within when it connects with the authentic Loving intent of another being, event, or circumstance—even a symbolic representation like a piece of art inspired by the divine connection with the God of Creation in us all. Even the resonance felt from the strands of a cello played with a Loving heart connects us all with that same spark of divine expression commonly held throughout humanity. Some would call such resonance grace, the grace that releases the common understanding of the Loving Way inherent in each of us. To me resonance is the Ultimate Intimacy, within ourselves and with God and all our brethren. Resonance is the connection that reminds us once again of that Truth for all, and that Truth is *the path* for all, *and the end*, all in the Oneness It is.

"Thus clarity and purification come down to making a choice of how one wants to consciously see life: either out of rationality or of Truth. The former, without the guidance of Truth, presents us with the way of living that can best be described as merely coping with all life offers: a life of separation and all the pain which emanates from that misinterpretation of Truth. The latter, Truth, presents the way of living that celebrates all Life offers. By living fully, celebrating Life to the utmost, one is filled with gratitude for the gift Life simply is. This gratitude converts one's vision and reality as the grace which is our sufficiency in all things. Grace is that which balances our energies at all levels, so our bodily chemistry is rebalanced in ways that enrich our being and maintain our eternally youthful character. It is balance that converts our personalities to ones filled with the joy and peace of a Life celebrated as the Essence of God each one of us is, each in our own unique style.

"Learning to discern between one and the other of these choices, and how Truth can lead to more sound rational behavior, is tantamount to seeing your sense of personal power as being in control of your life, of consciously seeing God as a truthful collaborator in celebrating all Life is. On the other hand, seeing Life through the lenses of personal force would not only continue one's life on the path of coping it is on, but could only end up in the collective consciousness reflecting such a devastating process, impinging upon all it impacts, which, in all reality, is every one and thing. On the other hand, when we go within and listen to the still small voice that speaks only Truth in any given situation, we learn to live our Truth in each instance. The more we collaborate with and obey the divine breath of those angelic whispers, the collective consciousness is increasingly converted to that same divine energy. It, too, will eventually manifest only divine Essence throughout our entire being.

"Instead of investing in a seemingly endless, impossible task of cleansing one by one all the contaminants from our physical, mental, and spiritual beings, we need only to learn essentially one thing: to consciously make ourselves fully present with the collaborative God within and obey the Truth that inevitably resonates from that sacred inner sanctum. We will thus be led on every step of our journey, led truthfully and intimately to that which is for our Highest Good and only that. We all know our inner Truth when we see it. Our inner Truth resonates. It just feels *right*, and peace infills, surrounding the issue or concern, dissolving such elements into the ethers beyond. All one needs to say to oneself in any given instance is this: 'I know in my heart what is the right thing to do, so I'm going do that and only That. Now!' Or you can go within in the spirit of wonder and be awed by God's response to your presence. When we take the first intuitive response as our Truth in a given situation, this is the highest good we can bring to any circumstance or condition. It is only when we contaminate that Truth with rationalization or justification that we mess it up, engendering doubt and angst, which invariably lead us to a rationalized injustice in Truth's stead. Either way, this is the correspondent energy we give off, both within and without. Yet again we arrive at the focal point of choice.

"In any situation, then, whether it deals with our polluted streams, the attitude we have toward another or some group, or the fear we feel in moving forward, we need not be concerned with the right thing to do. All we need do is develop the capacity and the discipline to ask within and follow obediently, no matter how unusual the answer might seem in the moment. Truth is Truth, no matter what it may seem, how it may appear to us at the moment. This is the way of the collaborative God, the way of our common sacred Essence that resonates as the Truth it is.

Truth, our inner Truth, then, is the universal anti-pollutant. Truth is that which leads us, moment by moment, to take those steps, no matter how small or large they may seem, in resonance with our Highest Good and the Highest Good for all concerned. The ultimate result is that the streams of Life, whether of water or blood, whether of physical, mental or spiritual being, are cleansed, purified, and returned to their most natural state of energetic being: Loving Creation personified.

"Now let's investigate for a moment the attitudinal impact on how we view life. It all relates to heart energy. How about these expressions: 'My heart's just not in it today.' 'She has such a warm heart!' 'What a cold-hearted person he is!' 'Take heart, man, everything's going to be just fine.' 'What a hardhearted Hannah!' 'That warms the cockles of my heart.' 'He wears his heart on his sleeve.' 'Ya gotta have heart, man!' Are these, and more, not the expressions of attitude coming from the heart? None of these are felt with our physical senses, but rather from the resonance each has within. Obviously they also point to the emotional component of the heart as that which has enormous impact on our body and Soul.

"It has been said that God created humans so God could feel the emotions expressed, which, of course, means that they *are* to be expressed—and not hidden or repressed. Suppression of emotions creates an inner tension in the body and Spirit, and establishes bodily chemistry to correspond with that particular level of stress. The longer the suppression lasts, the more out of kilter is the chemistry. One doesn't have to go much further to understand that this is not a healthy condition, either spiritually or physically. So attitude is yet another ingredient for determining how each cell is being cast to the world, for living in the world.

"We are led around the world from day to day by how we envision life, by our perspective on it, both widely and specifically. Our heart energy precedes us as it surrounds us, interacting and picking up signals from whomever and whatever we come into contact with. Those can be interpreted either by our five senses through the brain, or through the heart sensors. The former is characterized by rational thought about what has been felt or seen. On the other hand, the heart's sensors let us know the Truth about each interaction. Rational thought is what we need to be correct in our interpretation of what's going on around us. What we pick up through resonance in our heart is the Truth of any situation. This Truth is what transcends differences and rationality. It goes much deeper than rational thought, many layers deeper, as Leonard Cohen says, a thousand kisses deep—and then some.

"Opening up the heart lets one see beyond the apparent differences of things like skin color, gender, religious choice, sexual preference, and geographic location, for heart energy is inclusive in its interpretation, while the brain is exclusive, selective, and even judgmental. The heart translates in a way that brings inner joy and peace, that which can be applied in times of war, unrest, chaos, divisiveness and rancor, and, of course, to every day-to-day situation. Just remember that out of the chaos of coping with life comes the divine order of Loving, even though we sometimes have to be jolted to the core before we can shift our direction. It all stems from a heart open to divine intimacy, found at the core of authentic Loving. Compassion is its name.

"Reading heart energy, resonance felt with the deeper elements of the world—beyond rational to the depths of God's Word for each of us—is something to develop, and it can be. It is not something one needs to make sense out of before putting it out into the world. Simply putting the untarnished Word out into the world affords the opportunity for resonance, both within ourselves and others, to interpret or translate for oneself. Resonance is God's connection between us all being heard within each. The resonance of one bumps into another, with the same kind of power that approaches the 'bump in the night' that enlightens our heart and Soul with the Truth of the moment. Our job, at least in part, is to be a speed bump, to slow ourselves down, and others by our example, so that we all can hear—really feel—the resonance within that informs the Truth. This is the real knowing space, the heart space that knows all, that which expresses only the Truth of the Word when resonance bumps it free.

"As we all know so well, Life requires making choices that expand us, not setting limitations on one's thinking regarding the world of possibilities. Being open to God's way in all, no matter what it may temporarily seem, is the way to inner peace and joy. Otherwise some humans and other entities may appear to be less than others. This cannot be, for all are equal in God's eyes. Words, words, words. Has man not yet understood that God's Word is not what is written or spoken, but only that which is heard in the solitude of the human heart, in individual relationship with God, and heard as resonance felt? This is the God within that is spoken of in the scriptures. I Am is not what others call God, but what I Am, or to put it another way, what God Is. God expressed as I Am is in each of us no matter what else we believe about God. No one can change what God Is, or where God is. To believe otherwise is making of God something God is not.

"Now, how is it that one hears, sees, or feels? By his or her human senses? Yes, but only for material matters. For matters spiritual, or to hear, see, and feel spiritually, to discern spiritually, that must be done in one's heart. The heart assimilates all that deep meaning throughout each cell by circulating resonance via the blood system. This is the Life that flows into every single cell, filling it with the inner knowing of Oneness. This is what links humankind together as One and that which makes it foolish to separate one from the other. Each is constructed of the same divine Essence; each has the same cellular structure; each has DNA—and all the things not yet discovered.

"Yet some still want to make one person different from another? Nah! Each is but God's idea, God's Essence, God's matter and substance uniquely displayed, just as trees do that, roses do that, and birds do that. But a tree is a tree, a rose a rose, a bird a bird, no matter what their individual description. Down deep we all know the same about Life. It's just that some feel safe only in their intellect and so must deal with life in a more limited, rational fashion. We need only to practice going to our heart and asking but one simple question: 'I wonder what is right in my heart about this given situation?' Invariably if one tunes into the heart, the spiritual answer, the only correct one, will appear—instantaneously. For those of strong intellect and/or ego, the real answer will be doubted, even transgressed, for it will be foreign to their way of thinking. Then the fight begins as to which is right. There is only one really correct answer, and that is what comes from within each person. The heart knows.

"Much, though not all, of what you hear from the various religions is inaccurate. The only real thing that is accurate is what comes through each heart in relationship to God. If this is translated to teach others, then this is what is correct, although it is not necessary to teach a doctrine of such things. The only doctrine to teach is for each to go within, to the seat of their own heart, for their answers—all of them. Practice this now, so you can say with Authority that this is the way. Eventually each will come to this, and when this is so the collective nature of it will transform Life as most have come to know it. Then heaven and earth will definitely be one and the same, much as it will be for each individual as he and she masters this way. This is the way of the Christ, the Loving Spirit that guides us, and that of which Jesus spoke. You will find the expression in scripture that will verify this. Be especially attentive to this now—and be careful lest you perpetrate and perpetuate a house of consciousness divided against itself.

"Now to put a slightly different torque to these understandings, let us be undergirded by the knowledge that over a period of approximately seven years all of our old cells are replaced by new ones. Just place this understanding alongside the potential this overall shift has for revamping our entire energy system. Because we know the variety of entities that impact on our energy and that they each effect how that energy transforms our cellular structure for better or worse, we can come to manage the input of energy and thus radically overhaul our entire cellular structure. Of course, that includes the purity of the energy that modulates within all our life support systems, including the one most often forgotten, our spiritual support system.

"We don't get to arrange all of our cells on the starting line so that in seven years we have modified all at the same time. No, cells come and go on their own timetable, but as each releases its life for its replacement, the opportunity is there to influence its substance in very different ways than most previously would have done. Where we once may have clouded our cellular structure with the energy of worry and fret, with angst and concern, with anger and vengeance, and with depressive thinking and its aftermath, we now, in each waking moment, have the opportunity to change the way we think about Life and what it brings us. Beginning, let us say, with the notion of divine order, and knowing we don't tamper with its natural course for long, we initiate the process of letting go of worrying about things over which we have no control. Then we need only focus our attention on the only things we can control: our thoughts, ideas and beliefs, which form our perspective about any given situation.

"Now we're back to choice again. Simply put, we have a choice—and only we can make it—over how we respond to what Life coughs up into our midst. We can choose to see it in any way we wish. For example, we can choose for ourselves the role of victim or martyr, creator or collaborator. We can take responsibility for all our actions or blame the world for all that happens to us. The single most important thing to remember in all this is that negative response generates a negative cell makeup. It engenders bad juju, bad chemistry, which then degenerates various parts of our physical makeup, and with it our emotional, psychic, and spiritual makeup. One influences the other always. A positive, sunny outlook about Life, genuinely so, makes for a far more wholesome response on all levels of being. Visualizing our cells and Life in general filling with healing light, much of it in the form of inner enlightenment that inspires and uplifts, is an extraordinarily powerful antidote to a current cellular configuration that comes from a depressed mental state and all its stress-driven energetic deficiencies.

"Over a seven-year period, more or less, we can transform our lives from one that speaks to a lost Soul mentality to one of sacredness, a Soul filled with passion for one's destiny and compassionately connected to our planetary collaborators. As this transformation unfolds, our body chemistry begins to change for the better, and with it, our mental outlook brightens. Life begins to take on a much healthier glow; our Life's purpose begins to focus; and we are led to all we need to know to continue the journey with zest and zeal. Indeed, the riches, the gifts Life is, unfold before us day in and day out. We build on this new foundation of goodness until our old habits of thought and demonstration are left in the dust. Our belief system changes before our eyes. We are led to books and programs and new acquaintances and ideas that resonate deep in our heart space, so we come to know, and routinely practice, resonance as our guiding light.

"This may move you to inquire: 'But what is the process I must use to arrive at this new cellular structure, this new way of living, this new attitude about Life? It sounds like a long and arduous process.' Very simply, there isn't one. It's simply about acknowledging the resonance you have with this as Life's most important commitment: fidelity to what you already Are. Once you have genuinely declared this to the world, the world begins to feed you the Word you need on your journey. It's then only about listening, really listening, to the resonance within as it informs you of your path, moment by moment, day by day, throughout eternity. Hearing spiritually and seeing spiritually are essentially the same thing: a deep inner feeling, a resonance with the God connection that is right for us at any given moment. It is the purest form of intimacy. This can come about only by paying attention to resonance in complete presence of the moment. This is the wind that blows the divided house down, and which sweeps away all the falsehoods that held this straw house up in the first place.

"This does not mean that you must meditate 24/7. What it does mean, however, is that you *must connect with Life* 24/7. You cannot be floating off somewhere out of ego need, but must rather be present to each moment as it appears, and listen to it with discernment—listen for the resonance with its Truth for you. Then you *must be obedient* to what the resonance tells you. To be sure, old habits connected with doubt and worry and fear will enter, or at least try to enter. Your only job at this point is to stick to your path of obedience no matter what you are told or feel to the contrary. Truth is Truth, and nothing can destroy or modify it—providing you live according to it. Healing thyself is the operative sense of all this, and never has it been more true, nor more necessary, than now.

"A quick, rather humorous story about Truth showing up. Generally I operate on the belief that Life is nothing but metaphor whose purpose is spiritual. The only way I know how to explain it is that my pragmatism is rooted in spirituality, not materiality, although my approach does send some of my friends into a frenzy. Some time ago I had begun to notice that the tires on my front-wheel drive vehicle were spinning as I pulled away, even ever-so slowly, from a stop sign or out of a parking space. I resonated on some level with the spinning tires each time. Just a few days after I had purchased new tires to take care of the spinning, to get a better grip on the highway, or so I thought at the time, during a conversation with one of my sons I was momentarily bemoaning the feeling of being stuck, to which he replied: 'Sounds to me like you're spinning your wheels where you are, Dad.' To which I responded, 'Yep, and I got new tires so I could get a grip on life and move on in the right direction for me.' Resonance affirmed!

"Yes, I had earlier picked up on the inner Truth that I was currently spinning my wheels, and needed to get a grip on the next leg of my journey. My automobile, my means of getting around in life, had spoken metaphorically to me in that regard. Then to have the absolute affirmation of that Truth surface in a conversation seemingly unrelated to that feeling is Life's mystery unveiled. This pattern was more recently affirmed when on a short trip I noticed that a light would go on on my dashboard every time I pressed on my brakes. On one level I simply knew that a bulb needed replacing. But you know me by now. I also understood that contained in the first message was another even more important message for me. I had been moving through life at a blistering pace and hadn't taken time to gain perspective. I wondered out loud what this signal was now telling me. In an instant I heard: 'When you put on your brakes and slow down, you'll be enlightened.' I laughed my way into enlightenment the rest of the way on my trip as I slowed down my mind and pace to obtain the True perspective I needed at that moment. What a gift life is! Listening for resonance is the key. Operating from the Truth of the resonance is the door that opens to the next layers of unfoldment that Life affords in all its giftedness.

"I am sure you all have heard of ADD by now, Attention Deficit Deficiency. A friend recently inspired me to follow his lead in coining a new term, IDD: Inspiration Deficit Deficiency. The only cure for lack of inspiration is to follow the journey conducted by our heart's leading. Going to the heart, just as going to the word processor when one wants to write, produces the only ingredient necessary for enlightenment, healing, and renewal. Once there, inspiration greets us—the divine guidance that takes us quickly and absolutely to the Truth for us in any given situation. Too simple? Too? No. Simple? You bet! All of Life is just that when we let it be so.

"That's what Life Is: simplicity demonstrated through the likes of you and me. God's Essence uniquely expressed through each of us is our authentic nature as sacred Lovers of the divine. This is our True nature that makes it possible for us to see the sacred in the mundane with indelible clarity. The only place that this vision can be found is in the deep recesses of our heart space. Indeed, it is time to get to the heart of the matter. As that marvelous melody of years long since past goes, 'Ya gotta have heart. All ya really need is heart.' Never has a lyric been so Truth-filled. Never has its impact been more profound.

"Jesus knew this and used this to heal all who were touched by his Loving presence. Now is the time for us to emulate the same as our way of Being. Yes, and greater than this will you do, all of you, for this is a theological mythology that can and does serve Loving-kindness, and heals all touched by it, no matter who it is that is applying it to Life's offerings.

"Well, there you have it. I hope that this puts the frosting on your spiritual cake for you. Let me summarize in very brief form what we have discovered today, as a way of wrapping it all up in a safe container that you can open up at will. Having reinforced what we have reopened to our understanding, what Truths we have re-membered with, let me once again help you understand that you had no real need to record all this with instruments from the outside world. Because of the resonance you have felt with that which is your Truth at this time, you now understand, I am sure, that you can and do know of the vehicle for continuing to do so. By staying in touch with resonance as you traverse the planet you'll be regularly in touch with your Truth as it comes to you.

"Also, if you want to recall anything about a particular topic we covered today, all you *really* need to do is ask yourself this question: I wonder what I already know about this topic? Then just be a person in waiting while you go about your normal business. Or sit in a meditative state simply waiting for some Word to show up. After all, God already knows what you need to know and will furnish it through the Holy Spirit in the very best way for you. Continue on your journey using this simple vehicle. Each time you need guidance, which is every time you want to do or think something for yourself, just go within and declare your wonderment. Then wait in awe for what you know is sure to come. This is the tack that unites the house of consciousness by exercising the choice to go only within for Truth on each occasion Truth is called for.

"Just in case the main points of this mythology of Jesus have slipped your mind, permit me to briefly summarize their importance. The main point is that we have, through earthly domestication, come to see ourselves through cloudy lenses. What I mean by that is that what most of us think of ourselves is a great underestimation of our value and worth, both to others and ourselves. Secondly, we are not separate from our God of Loving, but rather created exactly in that Loving image and likeness. That alone unites us in our Oneness, as Loving Essence. When we look at the characteristics normally applied to God (Loving) we tend to think that they are beyond our ability to portray them. Yet when we look closer at these attributes, these Loving applications to our lives and within our relationships, we find that we, too, do indeed apply them daily. For those we either haven't been aware of, or find ourselves lacking in application, we can begin anew today to be as thoroughly Loving as we wish, in the perfect image and likeness of Loving.

"We now know, too, that when we fall in love with Loving as our way of life, Loving becomes our way, our Truth, our light into the world of everyday experience. That is, Loving becomes the screen upon which we focus Life, rather than casting the darkly configured drama onto our screen and having that consume us. Creating Life Lovingly, and thinking about Life that way, affords us with the continual opportunity to expose our darkness that we formerly may have hidden, from fear of its exposure. By living Lovingly we have found that it is safe to expose our supposed darkness, and as it comes into the Loving light we find it to be not darkness at all, but rather behavior that simply informs us as to what we can do Lovingly in its place. Thus we avoid a constellation of behavior that could manifest in ways deleterious to our health—mental, spiritual, and physical—and even to those around us. By expressing Lovingly as our Life's Loving purpose we find that our attitude improves dramatically, and as our attitude becomes more openly Loving our body chemistry changes just as dramatically, and we look, feel, and act more youthfully. Joy fills our hearts, and peace, instead of obsessive compulsion, fills and propels our minds.

"We find, in thinking about the parables in a new light, that when we are attentive to the God in others in their moment of need, we are full collaborators in what can be instantaneous healing. How many times have you intuitively felt the need to call someone only to have them respond that they were just thinking about you—only to have a conversation that helped in some simple, yet profound way, for both of you? How many times have you wanted someone to just listen to you—not fix you—but simply pay attention to your perceived needs? And how many times have you done so for others, being fully present to the call from another for help? Have you ever heard yourself saying, "Now I see what you mean," or "That's the first time I've heard it said that way, or "I'm just dead on my feet from all this work"? I am convinced that, to a large degree, this is exactly what Jesus did. He read people's energy, their day-to-day calls for help, and helped them see and hear in different ways than those to which they had become accustomed. He raised them from the dead, relieved them of the kind of perspective that crippled them. He knew that they indeed were ill in the ways they saw Life and their way in it. And he helped most by reframing their perspectives about Life, their ways of perceiving it, so they were freed of their burdens. Indeed, on the yoke of Loving presence, out of their burdens came enlightenment.

"The point here is not that Jesus alone could do these things, but that you and I also do such things regularly, both for ourselves and for all to whose call we Lovingly respond. Yes, these things you do. Even greater do you do when you permit it of yourself, instead of wallowing in self-pity or victimization, or merely being stuck in the mud of a murky mythology that keeps us seemingly as less than the worst among us.

"When we find ourselves returning to our primary nature as Loving Essence we begin to see others more and more like ourselves, in the image and likeness of God. The more this becomes our vision, the less fear we have of others, the greater our respect and compassion for them becomes, and the appearance of differences between and among us seems to melt in the warmth of the Loving way. It is then that we begin to feel the amelioration, even disappearance, of feelings of separation between and among us. Those whose skin color is different from ours, whose gender and gender preference, religion, heritage, age, physical condition, or ideas are different from ours cease to be a burden for us. Instead, those appearances come to inform us about our real feelings and how we might modulate them to be more Loving, and how we can come to simply agree to disagree, without judgment, retribution or revenge. It is in this Oneness of Spirit, seeing all others as we are—One with God—which we come to respect the dignity of all and treat all completely Lovingly as our new way of Life.

"We have come to understand that God's purpose is to Lovingly Create. This does not mean that God sits in the clouds somewhere like Santa Clause to give out gifts of our choice or desire. God expresses God's Love to us by fulfilling the promise to give you all you need to fulfill your convictions, where it is you have placed your faith—either positively or negatively. God's laws are not applied selectively, that is, here and not there. A law is a law and must apply across the board. So if you are placing your faith in some fear, let us say of some disease, and you do not replace that conviction with something positive, then as long as you harbor that fearful conviction you are liable to contract that disease. Indeed, your dominant thoughts *are* your contracts with God. You will need to remember that even if you think you are placing your faith in some Loving idea, if you have severe doubts about it coming about, it will be the doubt that will overrule in the world of creation, and the Loving idea will have been snuffed out like a candle after supper. It is imperative that we clear our minds of any doubt that God will create all, so that when we commit our convictions to a particular choice that will benefit mankind, it will not only have every chance of being demonstrated, it can do nothing but that. Here again choice comes into play, this time at the heart of all we create in collaboration with God.

"When we can come to see ourselves in the likeness of Loving Essence and focus with all we are on that image, Life changes for so much the better. When we can come to see that with every thought, every statement, every connection with another, and with every action taken, we are creating something. All we need to be able to do is discern whether each of those creations is or is not coming from the Loving intent. Then we simply need to make up our minds about which world we want to live in: either a world of ecstatic Loving expression—or one which exemplifies worry, concern, angst, fear of the past repeating itself, feigned paranoia, self-pity, victimization and all the ills that pertain thereto.

"Let's reframe this one last time. Those of you who are Christians will recall the answer Jesus gave to Peter when he asked the Master why the fig tree he had cured had withered away. Jesus responded with, 'Have faith in God...That whosoever shall say unto this mountain, be thou removed, and be thou cast into the sea; and shall not doubt in his heart, but shall believe that those things which he saith shall come to pass; he shall have whatsoever he saith.' All of you will recall, I am sure, my earlier comments about how stories get distorted in translation. To begin with, in the original language, 'Have faith in God' is really meant to be 'Have God's kind of faith.' And what is God's kind of faith? God's kind of faith is faith placed *entirely* in the idea to be manifested. Without that kind of focus, that kind of intention, and that kind of conviction, none of us would be here today. Nor would anything else. This is the kind of conviction, the kind of faith—God's faith—that is spoken to later in the above message from Jesus. He says one shall not doubt. Shall not doubt where? In one's head? No. In one's heart, where, when one believes with all his heart, one creates that to which absolute faith is committed. This simple statement of Jesus is the key to living and Loving Creatively, and that to which we can commit; instead of letting Life create around us, with us seeming to be life's victim. It is the sacred ideas that come to us, which we hold and honor and ennoble as sacred by expressing our absolute faith in them, without doubt, that composes the 'Kingdom Within.' Yes, 'Seek ye first the Kingdom of God, and all the rest will come to you.'

"At this time in Life the choice is rather simple for me. I have only two ways from which to choose. The way I choose is to free myself for a Life filled with a joyful heart and peaceful Mind by intending and acting out of my most natural aspects of self: Loving Essence. Given the changed perspective we can create about Life, that which has crippled us in some way can now be healed in the continual process of Lovingly Creating Life in ways we have not always seen but now can really be. In sum, as the age-old tune once told us, let's choose to "accentuate the positive, eliminate the negative." And come alive Lovingly.

"Whenever we make this latter choice we are rendered complete, as we were originally created to be but can now finally see for ourselves. As such we can share our complete selves with other complete beings, rather than looking for something or someone else outside of us to complete us. At last we arrive home: at home with ourselves, intimately in the company of God within—and the God in all. It is when we come to Intimacy within, with ourselves and with God, that we can live day-by-day in Intimate connection with all whom and with what we come in contact. A new world order will thus be created, one in which Oneness of purpose and Creative Loving demonstration are most naturally the cause and effect of all being. We can live in a new order in which all pain and misery is eliminated, where all are cured of erroneous self-concept, where instead of being self-reliant, all are God, or Loving-reliant. Amen I say to that.

"This is a mythology of Jesus that works for me. It is a spirituality of the Christ, as it were. To be sure, it will be refined over time. Perhaps it will even be junked totally in favor of another, a Truth even closer than this mythology now appears to be. This I know for sure: I want to stay open to the possibility of such a mythology imparting its Loving ways to me. To deny its presence will only limit my spiritual growth and render me closed, or dead, to the world of divine reality. Instead, I choose the openness that provides for continual understanding of my spiritual being and its possible manifestations. But for now I celebrate the Loving Essence that feels most natural for me to express, and I invite you to join me on the Way, expressing this Truth, throughout all of Life. For Jesus said he (Loving) was that, as is God (Loving): indeed, Loving is the way, the truth, and the life. Loving creatively expressed is the nature that unites us all as One. Therefore, so must we be. And so it is."

Christo steps away from the podium for a moment to gather himself. He feels a sudden surge of sadness that this gathering is about to end. He has linked so closely with the group that it has captured him more profoundly than he recalled ever before feeling.

After taking several deep breaths and then reconnecting with the participants, he speaks again, gently, with a deeply appreciative tone in his voice: "I cannot thank you enough for coming to this gathering today, for providing me with the opportunity to bask in your divine presence. Even more important, I thank you and praise you for giving yourself the opportunity to see yourselves as you really are. I hope you leave here with a very different view of what you are and your worth to all who accompany you on this journey. I hope that you have come to see the goodness you are, instead of that shadowed personality you have allowed yourself to think you are. I hope that you will do your level best to connect with your God within regularly, for God is always here, it is only we who are afraid to see what that means about us. And I hope that you will now feel confident enough to remove the blinders from your eyes so you may finally truly see, and remove the impediments to reframing your life, so you can truly hear and know. Finally, I pray that you will allow yourselves to merge with the God in all so that peace may finally be a reality and the pain of separation may be forever erased.

Christo pauses one last time and listens within. "I want to ask you one last question: How many of you feel called to do something different with your life as a result of answering the call to be here today? Raise your hands." Immediately, all but a few raise their hands enthusiastically. "Ah, I thought so," responds Christo. "Well, then, I want to share something about answering a call of this magnitude that will have real meaning for you. It comes from an extraordinary medical intuitive by the name of Caroline Myss. I'm sure that many of you have read her books and listened to her talks. This bit of wisdom comes from her book called *SACRED CONTRACTS*. Permit me to quote:

> 'If you do decide to follow an inner call and its unavoidable psychic ritual of separation, you have to withdraw your spirit from the magnetic field created by the collective power of your group's will so that you can organize

your own energy, much as a mystic or seer might withdraw to hear divine promptings—like Jesus going into the desert or Muhammad to the cave of Mount Hira. This process of birthing your own power requires that you put yourself first, even though this may appear to the outside world to be 'selfish.'

During your separation you will have to face the most narcissistic aspects of your ego, such as the shadow Child, who is concerned only with its own well-being and will try to scare you back into the fold. Your shadow Victim, meanwhile, revels in its victimhood and will entice you to feel sorry for yourself for ever leaving. The shadow Prostitute will urge you to sell out your integrity and your vision of true independence at the first opportunity. And the shadow Saboteur will play to your suspicions that you just aren't good enough to accomplish anything on your own. You will have to strengthen your soul identity until it is strong enough to eclipse all these fears. You are birthing your power of individual choice, increasing your potential for insight and for opportunities serving your highest potential. In dealing with the shadows, you ready yourself to accept full responsibility for the management of your spirit and the consequences of your choices.'

"Now isn't she right on with what we have learned today? Are these shadows not similar in nature to those of which Jesus spoke when he spent forty days and forty nights in the desert? And what did Jesus say to them, represented by the symbolic devil? 'Get behind me, Satan!' We have learned the very same process here today: to face our so-called demons and place them behind us, so we can fill our spiritual coffers with something much more healthy. It is something we must do if we are to honor our sacred contract faithfully. This is compassion Lovingly expressed for us, and obedience to the call, all in one.

"Let me emphasize that just as Jesus faced the demons that he knew he must in order to answer his heartfelt call, this calling you now hear—the one you must follow if you are to serve your very own highest potential—so is this your opportunity to develop all we have spoken of today to the fullest capacity. Remember the words you have just heard from our sister Caroline as you traverse this path in resonance with the Truth each of you can now hear within. You are not alone and never will be. You are carried on God's bridge of Loving compassion until you become that bridge yourself. You surely will be that. And so it is. Just as it was with Jesus, so is it for you in that same Oneness of Spirit. You see, in this way, too, you and the Christ Spirit are One.

"Travel with care, for each of you is a most precious avenue for rectifying the ills of our beloved planet. I have every confidence that you will now avail yourselves of this opportunity and I am just as confident that you will do your

God proud. Many leave programs like this fearing that when they go back into the 'real world' they will soon forget all they've learned, or that what they have learned simply won't work 'out there.' I want you to leave today with the sure understanding that the real world is not 'out there,' but rather that the 'real world' is that still small voice within that you carry with you everywhere you go. When you traverse the planet with this attitude of heart, this perspective on what Life is really about, you become the prayer that blesses all you touch. And the house once divided against itself will finally unite as One. Indeed, you are the prayer with which we end our session today.

"Thanks to your generosity and the personal information you have shared with us, you shall be hearing from me in a few months." Christo pauses and then, taking a long deep breath, he says one last heartfelt: "Namaste—and God speed." The crowd starts to applaud, and then, in perfect understanding of how inappropriate that would be, in spontaneous unison they send back to Christo a gentle, loving, "Namaste, Christo. God speed." They linger only to taste the beloved connection for just a few more minutes before quietly filing out of the arena all aglow with thoughts of what they had come to know about themselves and one another.

Christo stands at the podium until the very last of the participants has parted, his sense of sufficiency complete. Merged totally with his God within, he wears a warm smile, a glowing heart, and a twinkle in his eye as he greets his Followers. "Well," he asks, chuckling with glee, "are your baskets filled with the crumbs left over from the feast—or are you still hungry?" With aplomb, he leads them to the banquet that had been prepared by the sponsors. It is a simple meal, complemented by the finest bread and wine. Christo privately wonders if his disciples would be able to tell the difference now.

What Now?

This personalized e-mail or letter was sent from Christo Sahbays to each participant three months after the first gathering:

Dear David,

Namaste. I hope all is going well with you and yours. I want to thank you once again for your contributions and the personal information you have shared with me. These make it possible to communicate with you from time to time.

By now I'm sure you are taking as gospel for living your life what you have come to realize from our recent gathering. You need to do nothing else but that in order to enhance life on this planet: living each moment in your absolute Truth. There is no requirement that we must fix others. To reinforce what I said at our gathering, there are essentially only three kinds of business: God's business, your business, and my business. Simply put, the only business to which I am to give energy is my business, unless invited to engage otherwise. If I give my energy away trying to do God's business, or your business, then who is "home" to take care of mine? Where do I then get the energy to take care of my own business if I have used it up elsewhere? It's no wonder most of us are tired most of the time, from spending our priceless energy where it doesn't belong. I have come to learn the hard way that my business is constituted by the limitations of God's call to me, and that alone. It is to this that I am to be obedient——and nothing else. What follows are a few reminders of how you can reinforce such a rich pattern of living. I offer them only as that. As is now usual for you, I am confident that only your own individual discernment will inform you of what is best for you.

If from time to time you take just a moment to review what has come forth from our day together, but even more important, from your inner Authority within, you can continually reshape your personal theological mythology that speaks from the seat of your own Truth. Is there a framework that can help in this process? I'm sure that there are many, as many as there are inhabitants on the face of this planet, and even more, just for the creating. Here are several guidelines that may be helpful in discerning the correct path for you in designing a life of inner peace and joy. I offer these few suggestions and encourage you to develop your own means for shaping your continually evolving life.

1. Be sure you build into the process the means for regularly hearing your inner Authority on any issue, concern or circumstance. We are so well trained to ask someone else for help and to listen to us, and then we take the advice out of hand without even checking it out through our very own internal reflection. The more often we go within, not to the figments of the imagination that contain only those thoughts we have taken in from outside our Truth, but to our inner voice of Authority that speaks to us like a bump in the night, the better and better we will be able to hear that voice and eventually simply follow it as *the* Truth for us. No matter how strange Truth may sound in the moment, it will sound less and less strange as you become more and more accustomed to hearing its resonance in the depths of your heart.

We all have taken in so many directions for daily living, both explicit and implicit: from conversations to nonverbal clues; from what we have heard within but refuse to acknowledge; and from repeating something our parents or significant others have said or done. The simple truth of the matter is that we already know in our heart what we are to do in any given situation. We merely have gotten in our own way so we cannot see or hear the Truth when it is given to us within. We just need to s l o w d o w n our pace of living and the complexity of our thinking a good bit so we can have the space between the lines in which to read our Truth. It's so often true that what is on the lines is not the Truth at all. All too often it's only what we think, or what someone else thinks, is what we hear. The actions taken by another are often what's between the lines. When we take an appropriate amount of time to juxtapose one's words against one's actions, including our own, then we finally are able to gain the proper perspective for ourselves in the given situation. Without such a clear perspective we cannot see the forest for the trees and we make the incorrect decision for ourselves most every time. Some fun and even some good can come from such a distorted way of decision-making, but it doesn't really last or satisfy because it really isn't our Truth that has prevailed.

2. Some would have us believe that to make decisions based on our inner Truth only would be unabashedly selfish and self-absorbed, self-centered. The reality is that unless and until we *do* make decisions based on what is really True for us, the decisions are improper or incorrect for all concerned. If we make decisions based on fear of someone's view of us, pressure placed on us (real or imagined), hurrying so we won't lose the opportunity, or just because someone says we must, then the decision is rarely, if at all, correct for us. To be sure, making decisions in such a dysfunctional way more often than not leads to disaster for all concerned. On the other hand, if we make decisions from the inner feelings of "goodness," then we are taking care of ourselves as we are supposed to be doing. If someone objects to that, then what they are asking you to do is make decisions that correspond to what they think is right for you—and them—that often is a part of their hidden agenda. It is perfectly proper for each of us to make decisions that we know are right only for us, for such represent our inner integrity and self-respect. Such obedience to our inner Truth celebrates our dignity.

Decisions made first and foremost for our highest good represent the beginning of the process that leads us to love our neighbor as ourselves. If we cannot live in a way that allows for decisions to take us to the highest and best for us in any given situation, how then can we come into any relationship with our own integrity intact? In a word, impossible! It is only when we decide for our highest and best that we are living authentically, genuinely, with the highest respect for our own dignity. When we have learned to do this, then we must certainly understand that all others deserve the very same for themselves. We thus are honor-bound to respect their decisions and behavior as if these were our own. It is by respecting the rights of others that healthy collaboration is initiated and, if it continues, it can lead to the highest forms of intimacy on all levels of being.

3. The more one develops the skills and inner strength described in the items above, the stronger one's self-esteem becomes. As one's self-esteem grows, one begins to understand living life passionately and demonstrating compassion on the highest levels. If one operates out of low self-esteem, however, one can only come to the world seeing and acting with those lenses as the filter for their decisions. With high self-esteem comes the ability to continue the process of spiritual discernment, looking to one's inner Authority for answers of all kinds. On and on it grows.

With high self-esteem one begins to discern what one's real purpose in life is and how one is to create that from whole cloth. Without such information gained from spiritual discernment one is sure to career from pillar to post, looking to outside validation for such directions. One thing is for sure: when one listens carefully for the voice of inner Authority and clearly hears its clarion call, then the only choice becomes whether of not you want to what you know is True for you. So often the call seems foreign to the issue at hand, or even contradictory to the direction we've already begun. Foreign or not, when taken, one can rest assured that this is the very best decision for all concerned, because it has come from the Truth of one's spiritual Authority. A brief story will illustrate.

Once upon a time there was a man who had a deep inner calling to serve the homeless. Why, it matters not; he heard the call and knew he had to follow it. One day a friend visited him on his rounds and came to understand the enormity of his friend's calling. At a point along the way he said to his friend, "My gosh, John, your work here is endless. It seems so futile and such an inefficient use of your time and talents." "Ah," replied John, "now I see why you're having so much difficulty with me working here. You think my work is about futility and efficiency. My work is not about either of those. It's only about obedience to the call." Is the same not true about each of us?

Because our lives are about Spirit and not material, one cannot go wrong by living true to one's spiritual calling. This is the only place within which we are ever truly satisfied. This is grace personified and where we finally learn that it is God's grace that is our only sufficiency. Anything beyond that, meaning outside of spiritual sufficiency, satisfies only ego demand, or greed or gluttony or pride. But it cannot ever satisfy our call to our purpose that somehow feels empty without Truth governing it. Like an egg with no yoke, life without Soul becomes hollow and without substance.

4. We all have the capacity to be headstrong, to develop and maintain our convictions at any price, usually to our internal demise. There is nothing wrong with thinking through how we think and feel about certain of life's offerings. But life is so very complex, just like the human mind, and to think that one can have only right convictions about all matters is not only unrealistic. It is arrogant and prideful. Such does the emphasis on knowing, knowing, knowing perpetrate: answers are gained only from a head game of sorts. Yet the intellectuals would have us believe that this satisfies the pursuit of happiness. I would submit that while intellectual pursuit is important as a starting point, it is spiritual discernment gained through the likes of intuition and divine inspiration that informs us of the specific thought and action required for the integrity of our being.

As long as we treat our convictions simply as ideas to ponder and not as firm beliefs, they are easy to approach with alternative casts applied to them. However, when we become headstrong about certain concepts and turn them into hard and fast beliefs, we are quick to anger when they are challenged. The more challenged we feel the harder our head and the stiffer one's neck becomes in defense of them. Keeping an open mind and remembering to take all questions of importance to our heart for the answer are keys to authentic living.

The mind contains a myriad of information, much of it fear-related, especially when it comes to decisions about relations with others. When we enter life from the pit of our fear-filled mind, much of our decision-making will be fear-involved instead of lovingly freeing. When, on the other hand, we make decisions by inquiring of our fearless heart, our ego is cast aside and we are able to clearly see the highest and best solution for all concerned.

5. Another way to look at developing our own inner voice of Authority is to shed the masks of intellectual demand for more and more and take on a spirit of awe and wonder. This is about the attitude with which one approaches life's offerings. When we use intellect alone we are leaving out the deepest and most precious jewels of our wisdom. Why would one want to do that? More than likely it is because that is what the ego would have us do, and most of us have learned to obey our ego quite well. However, when we approach the world with an attitude of awe and wonder, what we really are committing to is to plunge to the depths of our being with a willing Spirit, a Spirit that allows for God's grace to show its way into our way—*as* our way. When we listen to life flowing through us without judgment, we are surrendering to a willingness to hear Truth from our depths, a Truth that resonates with meaning that far surpasses that of the intellect alone.

This is not to say that we ought to discard the intellect. Hardly. It merely means that we should use our intellect in service of our inner Authority and not the other way around. When we have discerned and developed the skill to do just that then our capacity for true, holistic, collaborative, and balanced living finally appears at our doorstep. All it needs is acknowledgment and exercise; practice, in order to become a new, far more authentic and truthful means of living for us. All those around us benefit in proportion to our commitment to living from our inner Authority, so the sooner we begin, the better life will be for all connected with it. After all, when we treat our understanding of God with awe and wonder rather than as the intellectual pursuit of that which cannot be determined through other than wisdom, we are honoring our path as true spiritual warriors.

6. It may well come to pass that as you are working on honing your skills to access God within that you begin to have some distracters to that process show up. The ego, for example, will be threatened by the potential for

replacement of its authority over you. Its major tool, fear, will begin to creep into your discernment process in the form of doubt and angst. Let me be absolutely clear and simple in suggesting the antidote to such interference: have no doubts, no angst. Say "no thank you" to both, just as Jesus did to the devils of his mind. Regularly utilizing this treatment on that which can hinder your evolution will pay handsome dividends. Faith placed fully in your impending Truth, and persistence in protecting your journey, will deliver Truth to you without fail.

7. If you are looking for a means that can take you to greater clarity in how you treat oneself and others, you might want to visit another of the offerings that has come through me, *FROM HUMAN DOING TO SPIRITUAL BEING; A Guide to Reclaiming Your Soul.* This is a conquest of moderate length that will take you to a keener understanding of the current condition of your self-esteem. If you decide to undertake this conquest as one means for becoming more spiritually discerning, be careful to go very slowly, and perhaps with a significant other, so you can reinforce the goodness that can come from such discernment.

I remain confident that as long as you continue to look within to your inner Authority for the Truth that takes you to your highest good in each moment life offers, you will soon see life as the eternal gift it is. I wish you well on your journey and hope to be with you yet again as we traverse this planet together for the good of all. In the not too distant future I will be sending along a brief piece that you should then be ready to contemplate. It even may serve as a foundation for our next gathering.

In any event, know that I believe in you and all you are. God speed.

In your service, I am,

Christo Sahbays

You Are God

This personalized e-mail or letter was sent from Christo Sahbays to each participant six months after the first gathering:

Dear Emma,

Namaste. I suppose that by now you are well on your way to living a life richly informed by your inner Authority. In case you are not yet so, this is not a sin, merely notice that you can return to doing so by simply recommitting yourself to a life of inquiring, one of visiting and trusting your inner Authority in a spirit of awe and wonder. "Your sins are forgiven. Take up your bed and walk—sin no more." Sound familiar? You bet it does. It may just be time for you to cast aside the bed you have made for yourself aside and construct a new way of life. Just change the way you think about what is truly valuable to you and exercise that. And don't go back to the old way: sin no more. Changing the way you think about life is what it means to repent: change what you are doing, what perspective you are bringing to life. And doing so without remorse, guilt, or shame, simply looking within to your inner Authority and getting on with life.

No matter where you are on your journey, the time has come to investigate a teaching that has the potential for taking you beyond where we left off last time we communicated. I have full confidence in your ability to fathom the depths. I'll come right to the point. I'd like you to consider something beyond what we know as the Truth that God is infinite, Omniscient, Omnipotent, Omni-present, Omni-active, at least in the literal sense. In the physical sense it is very difficult to see that God is everywhere present, is everything God created. But in a metaphysical sense, in the sense of thought, it becomes less difficult and more the Truth.

Let's start with the usually-understood expression of Godliness, a God that is featured as separate from us. Such a metaphysical configuration is laughable, and a sign of unadulterated vanity. It is vane to think of us as separate from God, or from anything God has created. We have come to understand that God creates all and that all God creates is of the same loving Essence, the same energy, thus of the very same substance. When we can finally come to see this for the Truth it is, we can then make the next leap: that one and all IS God. Is it difficult to imagine this lofty place: that you *are* God?

Be very careful to clearly discern what I have said here. I did *not* say that you are or I am *a* God or are *the* God. I said all *IS* God, which then mediates to mean, therefore, that I, too, *am* God—and that you, like all others, also are God. Let's think of this proposition in metaphysical terms. If all is the idea of God manifested into material form, then clearly one could easily come to understand life this way: "There is God, perfectly expressed as that leaf." "There is God, perfectly expressed as Daniel, or as Mary, or as that rose, that river, that sunset, and as that newborn baby." Each and all are perfectly manifest of the Loving Essence of God and, therefore, *is* that Loving Essence: God. This provides the true meaning of perfection: that all are manifest as the perfect Loving Essence that is God. You are that. I am that. All is that. Hence, "I am that, I am." On and on goes such perfect manifestation, such sacred creation, on into infinitude. God *is* infinitude! We, in our perfect state of image and likeness of God, also are infinitude uniquely expressed.

If you are having difficulty wrapping your head around such an idea, and I can easily understand how someone would be, let's give this a try. Look at any wooden object in your home. Let's say it's a coffee table. We call it a coffee table, but what is it, really? It is wood, formed into a coffee table. So you could justly say, even though some people might think you're weird for doing so, "there is wood, expressed as a coffee table." Although that is true to a point, for sake of convenience and economy of words, we shorten the expression of our perception of it to say, "there's a coffee table." Now let's go to the root cause of that coffee table. What's the very basic root (pun intended) of the coffee table? Asked in another way, of what does wood consist? Why the Essence of God, of course, just like every other thing on earth that has been made by God. Just like you and I are that.

Now just take this idea to the obvious conclusion, as if you were telling the *absolute* Truth: "There is God, expressed as that coffee table." This sounds ridiculous, I know, but that doesn't lessen the Truth of it any. Actually, it's absolutely okay to call a coffee table a coffee table, just as long as down deep inside you carry the meaning to be that everything is the

Essence of God expressed. Using commonly-held shorthand based in absolute meaning is akin to responding with a simple "thank you" to someone who says that your writing is brilliant, when you really know that you weren't the one who wrote anything. You merely got out of the way so the Holy Spirit could write through you. The best we can say is that were are a midwife that nurses birth into reality. You know the Truth of the matter, and perhaps the one who complimented you does as well, so it doesn't hurt anything to return the compliment with a courteous response instead of a longer explanation that might only confuse. On some level, all involved know the Truth of the matter, whether it is communicated openly or not.

The same rings true as we speak about life with declarations that this or that is God expressing Itself as this or that—or as you or me, for that matter. The shorthand doesn't hide the Truth from us. It's only a matter of using language and talking about ideas in an economical way, with fewer words. Just don't forget the real meaning for yourself and how that effects how you treat yourself and all that comes into your path. Until this becomes real for you, you might try the following each time this comes up for you—for example, when you may be having some difficulty with a situation or a relationship. Just say in your head, "There is God, expressing Itself as John," or something equally appropriate for the occasion. After a time this pattern of expressing Truth will have become ingrained, and you will automatically carry this deep understanding forward as a central thread that governs how you see life.

This understanding will guide your responses to what Life brings to you. What results will amaze you, so just give whatever it is a little time to settle into your consciousness. First, you must send your ego to another location, for if you do not your ego will contest this idea in a very big way, out of necessity, simply in order to survive. If you are God expressed as what you are then there is no room for the ego, either to run your life or to counter the Truth of the infinite purity of Godliness. Jesus said: "Whoever loses his life shall find it." Whoever loses one's life of living with limitation of thought—and thus being—whoever loses one's way of living that primarily serves one's ego-need, gains instead the limitless life of infinitude and immortality. Yes, "Whoever loses his life shall find it." Truly, this is so.

So, for just a moment, let yourself go into that space of complete solitude. Slow down your thinking and let yourself receive and accept the breath of your inner Authority. Soon you will come to resonate with this Truth, or you will not. If you do, it is Truth for you. If you do not, that doesn't necessarily mean it is not the Truth, perhaps only that you are not yet ready to accept this as Truth for you. Either is perfectly okay. Each of us is on our own path and when readiness strikes we will hear it in the depths of our heart, portrayed as resonance felt.

Obviously, I've asked you to accept this without any verification, other than what you can come to from your own inner Authority. Actually, that is the *only* place where you can discern the Truth—either of what I have proposed, or of any other Truth that is to guide you through life. Nevertheless, in order to begin to persuade those who continue to inform themselves by intellect alone, permit me to now supplement what I have asked you to do yet again: to go within. I do so by providing some additional information with which to plumb the depths. I do so not to convince you of this proposition that you are God, but rather to give you some information that you can test within for potential verification. Testing information this way is the *only* affirmation that brings Truth with it. The resonance we feel within validates Truth for what it is, just as lack of resonance renders it not—or, at the very least, keeps things neutral.

First of all, we know that faith, heartfelt conviction of an idea, is the most powerful leverage of creation. What we put our faith in is what shows up in our material world. If we exercise faith in hope, it is hope we shall manifest; if faith in lack, it is lack that will find its way to our doorstep; if in love, love it will be; and if in fear, it is fear that will show its face. You get the picture. If we think in terms of limitation, then it is that particular limitation that is our faith expressed, and that very thing that will show up as our life limited. If we think of God as separate from us, sure enough God will show up separate from us, including the sordid feelings that only separation from God, and thus from ourselves, perpetrates on our way of seeing and feeling. Such separation generates the most painful feeling of all, a distancing from our reality that tears at our sense of purpose and very being. If instead we go within and imagine life free from such limiting thought, we bring ourselves into harmony with the God within each of us, the entirety, the infinitude of it that we are. Then we have a very different feeling within. Do this as a meditative exercise, and you will see exactly that what I am telling you is the Truth for you—if you are yet ready for the Truth of what you *really* are.

By investigating within with God, our inner Authority, we soon find out that we resonate with *THE* Truth about God and ourselves. We find out as well that the only thing that really is disturbing to us is the *thought* that it might not be true, or that it would be arrogant or heretical to think such a thing. But the idea itself, absent the *thought* to the contrary, *does* resonate within, with absolute clarity. The bell of Truth tolls absolutely, cleanly and clearly, without reservation. Have you done it? Is this not the Truth? Take your time and simply be with this in the depths of your heart. For a time it may be rather earth-shaking in its dimensions. In fact, it definitely will be, until and unless you release the hold ego has on your way of thinking and you replace it with the only thing you know can bring absolute Truth to you: your full presence in God's company. With this in hand the Truth will be known to you and you can then start living it *as* Truth.

You see, we cannot serve two masters: God and mammon; God and earthly thinking; God and ego. As we have come to understand, there is only God, no God *and*...If there were God *and,* then God would be a God of separation. God is not about division or separation. God is about One-ness and absoluteness; all of God's laws are that. We cannot use part of God's law for one thing or one determination and not for all. So when we declare that life itself is about metaphor, is about metaphysics, is about the way we think and how that most assuredly manifests in physical form, then we must go with that and that alone as our life's purpose and way to fulfill-ment. To obviate that is to obviate the Truth for us. Of course, that, like all else in life, boils down to choice, in this instance a choice between being a house divided and staying the course with our inner Authority.

There is absolutely nothing inherently wrong with believing otherwise: for example, that life is only about the material realm. One way or another this too will eventually lead you to Truth for you. That is God's promise to us. The choice of how we want to live shows its face endlessly, perhaps until we come to see that there really is *no* choice at all. Once seen, Truth is simply to be obeyed. We surrender to Truth and let its innocence show us the way, knowing finally that Truth is all that exists. In this knowing, fol-lowed by our obedience to it and nothing else—for there really is nothing else—choice is rendered nonexistent.

This is what evolution is really about. Evolution is not the process of becoming something more and more grand physically: bigger, stronger, smarter, and healthier, at least not from the outside in. Evolution is about expanding our consciousness to eventually include ourselves in the realm of Godliness. Evolution is coming to grips with how we think about life, how expansive our thinking can become, until we can think of God and ourselves without limitation. How we view God is contained in how we limit ourselves. God to us can only be as large as we allow ourselves to be, and that perspective is restricted by the limitations we place on ourselves. If we can create as God creates, bring into this world as God does, heal as God heals, all by the limitless thinking we allow to flow, then the God we think into existence is also that large: without limitation. Thus God will show itself in that form instead of in the form of limitation. The expres-sion, NOTHING IS IMPOSSIBLE FOR GOD then becomes the Truth in our lives. This is not so because some god outside of us is creating some-thing *for* us, but rather because the Godly ideas that come through us are tantamount to first *cause,* and first cause is that which manifests as *first effect.* Truly, God and we *are* One in being.

Not convinced yet? If not, it may be only because you are still in ego-controlled space. Or may be influenced by what you have been told elsewhere. Remember, discernment can only be determined within each of us, not from those we hear outside ourselves. Let me voice this to you and see where it goes. Let's take the concept of infinity. Most use this term today to convey that which is impossible to conceive: all of everything, everywhere, free of time and space. Infinity is limitless, unbounded, innumerable, and eternal. This last term, eternal, is a term used more frequently by scientists lately to link science with the everlasting entity of immortality, the limitless being of Spirituality. Most scientists, at least those of my era, could not operate in the world of the unknown known as Spirituality. After all, religion has taught us that God is unknowable. Spirituality, however, is founded on the absolute Truth that God is all, and thus is not only knowable, but also everywhere present and infinite in its expression. Therefore, all of creation is found in the individual expression of God, divine idea made manifest.

Applying this to our discernment process, then, God is everywhere and every thing; infinity is everywhere and every thing. God is everlasting presence; infinity is everlasting presence. God is omniscient; infinity is all knowledge: it is eternal, immortal, never changing. This is God and what God and we are, providing we don't limit God, or ourselves, from thinking this as Truth for the world and us. Infinite knowledge or intelligence, then, is all there is. We, as part of the "isness" of life, also are that. It is one and everywhere and is the stuff of which all is created, us included. It is at our disposal, as rightful inheritors of God's Kingdom. As you know so well, this is not the material Kingdom, but the Kingdom within, the Kingdom of divine ideas, the immortal potential for creation of all that is good. Does any of this resonate yet?

Is it not coming to be understood within you that infinity is just another name for God? And that our heart is the Kingdom that contains all that is, to be used by us in creation's way? Test this simply by going to the depths of your heart for anything. Go your inner Authority and see what comes of your journey there. Then take this Truth you find there, the loving, creative idea that it is, and bring it to full consciousness. Then let this Truth become your conviction: your belief, faith expressed. Hold it there, without doubt or other form of fear, simply turning it over to God's grace for the exact creation it will become. That which we see with conviction is what will be.

From the Vedanta, the chief Hindu philosophy, comes this: "Not a part, not a mode of That, but identically That, that absolute Spirit of the World. And the personal self and the ultimate impersonal Self are one." From the Sufi: "...the difference of "mine" and "thine" and distinction of "I" and "you" fade away in the realization of the one Life that is within and with-out, beneath and beyond; and that is the meaning of the verse in the Bible, 'In Him we live, and move, and have our being.'" And from no less than Jesus: "Who hath seen me hath seen the Father." We now bring different meaning than the literal to such pronouncements: the Essence of what we are is One in being with God. The ideas that come to us are one and the same with God. Our thinking is One with God, and God's laws work with God and us alike in the infinitude of loving creation.

God is thus not separate from us, but rather *is* us. God manifests as all things, and we, therefore, are of that same Essence, God Essence. We—all of us, and all other living things—are of that same Essence. We all create endlessly, exercising the commonality of infinity's ideas as our own because they are all and one the same in their foundation and availability. By the lack of limitation we place on ourselves, or God, we thereby access and accept the divine intelligence, and hold it with conviction in order for it to manifest as that which we create in collaboration with God. Instead of holding ourselves as separate from God in all Its infinitude, we co-create out of the Oneness with God we are. Truly, then, no one can legitimately place a limitation on God. Because we are created out of identical sub-stance and with identical purpose, there is no limitation we can legiti-mately lay on ourselves, certainly at least not on the creation of whatever to which we give clear thought and unfettered conviction.

I'm sure that you know by now that you cannot, should not, take what has been proposed to you as gospel. Words and even logic cannot bring you Truth. Illumination, enlightenment by another name, can only come about for each of us by going within to hear those sacred whispers of Truth that inform us as that. Sit with these ideas for a time. Listen for them in the depths of your heart. Then form your ever-evolving meaning of God as you come to hear Truth for yourself. This kind of commitment is a com-mitment to your evolution, the evolution of your coming to Oneness with God and one another.

This is plenty enough for you to take within for now, perhaps too much even. Do with it what you will. In a few months I will send you a notice of the time and place where we can further investigate these and other ideas together, in harmony with, and in commonality of, God's loving Essence.

Until then, take good care of yourself, for you are a grand gift of God to one and all.

In Ashk, God's Love, and Haqq, God's Truth, I remain your servant,

Christo Sahbays

Spirit Noodles

This feature is introduced here to invite the reader's personal investigation (noodling about in spiritual ways rather than material) into her or his own beliefs and perspectives on life. Such investigation is tantamount to engaging and inquiring about life metaphysically, symbolically. The reader is encouraged to investigate these beliefs not for purpose of material enhancement, but rather to nourish one's spiritual perspective and insight. As we then come to grips with Truth within for ourselves, thus healing our perspectives on life, our body chemistry and functions also heal as our thinking and beliefs are mended.

Chapter I: Emptying the Old Wine

1. Identify some of the old wine within yourself that needs to be discarded. What are some of the beliefs that no longer serve you, that get in the way of a perspective you would now like to invite into your being?

2. What are some appealing perspectives on spirituality that engage you at this time? What resonates with Truth for you, for guiding your life right now?

3. Have you ever been inspired to write anything original? From whence did this inspiration come? Find a favorite passage in the Bible that has made you think of its meaning differently from the norm. Sit with it until you become inspired to write a perspective about it that speaks to your heart.

4. What meaning did you take from the poem, "Life?" Let yourself create a word message that speaks to you in a similar way, that is, that can be taken both personally and spiritually.

5. What is your personal mythology of Jesus?

6. How has it impacted your life to date?

7. In what ways has the mythology presented above raised any new possibilities in your mind? Did it generate any unusual thoughts and feelings?

8. Can you withhold judgment on the suggested theological course, or do you have definite feelings that now make it difficult to pursue a potentially new manner of dealing with life?

9. Define for yourself any benefit you can discern in shifting your view of Jesus and the religion created around his teachings. Any feelings of loss? Of anger?

10. Are there any facets of the Bible that you have found to be used in ways that seem contrary to the teachings of Jesus? How would you correct the perspective on such situations?

11. As you think of the Adam and Eve story, how does it now guide you to look at your own spiritual development?

12. How do you think people learned to act in loving ways before religious texts came on the scene? In your view, where did they get their guidance for living a fulfilled life?

13. What distinctions can you make between religion and spirituality? Describe which, or what kind of blend, would work best for you.

Chapter II: Hidden Meaning

1. What was your response to the episode regarding the use of senses to discern meaning? Discern which you use most to guide you in everyday life. Is it literal or metaphorical meaning?

2.   What meaning do you attribute to the story about the man at the pool? In what ways have you "made your bed," both religiously and spiritually? What desire do you have to change the bed-clothes?

3.   How do you handle expression of emotions within yourself? And by others? For example, how do you handle the energy that comes with anger or tears? Within yourself? And with others?

4.   Have you ever repressed feelings and had them vent on some deeper level than would have been the case if dealt with when you originally felt them? How might you deal with feelings as they initially surface?

5.   What does the term "grace" mean to you? How does grace show up in your life?

6.   How did the metaphorical explanation of the parable of Bartimaeus strike you? Did it change any perspectives you may have originally had about its meaning? What did you take away from it in the end?

7.   How did you receive the metaphorical explanation of Jesus' death? How did you relate to various aspects of the explanation? For example, the explanation of why Jesus did not answer any of Pilates' questions. Or, the explanation of the symbolism related to the cross itself.

8.   When you think about the choice of going within or without for your personal Truth, with which approach do you feel more comfortable? What do you see as the advantages and disadvantages of each approach? How are they complementary, if at all?

Chapter III: The Simple Life as Image and Likeness of God

1.   How would you describe the ways in which you express feelings? Do you come from a sense of shyness or openness? Do you wish otherwise? If you do, what can you do about it? Go within for your answer.

2.   Describe God in simple language. Now go within to find God and describe what meaning this has for you.

3.   What is your point of origin, your essence? How does and might this perspective effect how you live from day to day?

4. How do you define what you are? Is this different in any way from the roles you play? Which do you think would serve your self-image better—seeing yourself as a 'what' or a 'who?' Give some thought to how you might use your understanding of what you are to make relational changes in your life.

5. What was your response to the bird visualization? Do you think you could live using primarily spontaneous guidance from within and still survive? Be willing to consider living this way and give yourself permission to live this way for, let's say, one weekend away from work. Keep a diary of what happens and what your feelings are as you proceed. Compare this with how you feel when you live as you normally do. To what degree are you willing to make a different choice for your life?

6. How does the explanation of omniscience, omnipotence, omnipresence and omni-active strike you? Can you yet see yourself that way? How close are you, and what would it take for you to realize this Truth about yourself? Go within for the answer. "I wonder…"

7. In what ways do you see yourself in harmony with God as a deliverance of the Loving way?

8. How are you and God alike? Different?

9. How well do you relate to God defined as the Loving entity? In what ways are you identical to God in the expression of Love?

10. Define what it means to say that you and God are One. Meditate on this description and see where it takes you. For greater clarity record the imagery in your journal and sit with it for a few days before returning to it. Own whatever it is that comes of it.

Chapter IV: Living the Miracles We Are

1. What is your definition of miracles at this point? Are you yet a miracle? If not, what are some of the things you could do to assist a change in perspective?

2. What IS fear? In what ways does fear enter your life? What are some of the more subtle forms of fear that are disguised as something quite common? How can you work towards a new outlook about fear? What steps can you

take to use fear to overcome its power over you and your decision-making process?

3. Have you ever been "moved" to tell someone something but yet couldn't bring yourself to tell them? What was the result, both for you and the one you were "supposed" to inform? Have you ever informed someone you were moved to inform? What impact did it have? What does such prompting have to do with internal integrity? How can it make a real difference in your life?

4. How does contact with the world of Spirit fit into your thinking? Do you make any attempts to be with anyone in spirit? How has, or does, it impact your life? When someone dies to this physical dimension, are they forever out of our reach? If not, how can they be reached, and is this an appropriate thing to do? What are its benefits and detriments?

5. Are our stories to be held within, or shared? How does sharing our stories, our parables, help us and those with whom we share them? What real meaning do they have? How does sharing our stories relate to living with integrity?

6. To what degree ought we be available to our brethren, even if simply to faithfully listen to them? To what degree are we to advise them, make what we think are helpful suggestions to them?

7. What are some of the boulders you have tossed in your situational knapsack? How might you have saved yourself the burden of their weight on your yoke?

8. What does fasting mean to you? In what ways can you place the suggested perspective on fasting in your life?

9. How do you normally pray? Are your prayers usually answered? If not, why do you suppose that is so? Define for yourself what your prayer life would look like if you used the method suggested, that is, simply going within and listening for the "still small voice,"? By recognizing that it is you who *are* prayer.

10. Do you tithe? What would it take to change your perspective to a more inclusive one, like that which is suggested? What problems would it cause

you? What benefits are inherent in such a commitment? Upon what does your commitment to tithe depend?

11. In what ways are you and God alike as creators? Describe how you and God are collaborators in divine creation. Do you see yourself as divine? What would help create a new perspective in this regard?

12. To what or whom are you married? How devoted are you to that marriage? What distracts you from it?

13. On what kind of foundation was this marriage formed?

14. Define what "separation" means for you and how it appears in your life.

15. Describe the feelings that accumulate to being separated from a loved one or treasured thing.

16. What can you do to support yourself and others in their inalienable right for harmony instead of separation?

17. Identify any defensive mechanisms you use to protect against feeling separated, or from actual separation. How might you redefine your response to the potential for separation?

18. Describe some realistic steps you can take to engage loving-kindness within rather than creating separation without.

19. What is intimacy to you? How and where and when are you able to meet Intimacy on its terms rather than on your own?

20. How can you learn to see God in all, so you can embody harmony instead of the propensity for separation from others and things?

21. Construct an easily applicable process for moving toward harmony in all circumstances and follow it for a few weeks, reviewing it daily. Reward yourself for obedience to highest good, and modify your thinking where appropriate—without the self-condemnation that doesn't allow for that—and then commit anew.

22. Do you speak from your ego or heart? How do you express yourself when you wish to live only in your integrity? How do you access your integrity?

How do you feel when you act from your integrity? How can you sharpen this process?

23. What is the difference between believing and knowing the meaning of something? How does each operate in your life? What can you do to strengthen your inner being and the clarity of your journey?

Chapter V: Creating a New Spirituality; The Key to Coming Alive

1. What are some simple ways at home in which you can contribute to the elimination of pollutants to the environment?

2. How can you extend this commitment to a wider concern for a pollutant-free environment?

3. List a few things you're willing to commit to in the act of cleansing your emotional and spiritual environment. And the bed of your thoughts?

4. How can repositioning yourself in your relationships and where you live assist in bringing healing energy into your life?

5. Describe a program for gradually cleansing your physical being and list a few new habits to implement every few weeks in order to achieve your goals.

6. How can others assist you in your outlook about such matters?

7. In a quiet, uninterrupted setting, meditate on the vision you wish to achieve for a stress-free, tranquil existence. Ask whatever comes into view what the meaning of its entry means for you. Ask how you can help with this process of finding a new space within, and living it without.

8. What are some ways you can practice building resonance with that which can set you free from enslavement to rationalization and justification as means of coping with life?

9. Build the ability to listen within for your own Truth, and regularly practice hearing it in every kind of situation. Begin by finding a way of meditating that is comfortable for you and just show up for it without any expectations. Keep a journal of what, if anything, comes from such sessions. But

remember that just showing up is the most important ingredient. For without that, there's no relationship to build on—and no voice to listen to.

10. Describe how you can find your Truth when immersed in everyday life: in conversations, relationships, events, and circumstances. Again, record at the end of each day some of the most profound, yet simple, understandings about yourself and your relationship with life.

11. Over the next few weeks and months listen carefully for inner guidance related to new initiatives, new areas of endeavor, new learnings that beckon. Say "yes" to them, not as intellectual, ego-driven callings, but only to those that truly resonate within. Follow them for a time, recording how each enriches your life, purifies your energy. Be assured that resonance will take you there with all you need to reach an enlightened state in each.

12. Consider your definition of prayer in the context of God already knowing anything you could possible bring to bear (and bare) in the collaborative space with Its resonance. Describe what your new role could be and how you might initiate going about fulfilling it. Remember to be open to changes in the process that are dictated by the clarity of resonance between you and God.

13. Keep a weekly log in which you record what is happening to your life and how you are responding to it. Make notes about how you might change your thinking towards what unfolds over the week. How can you work toward being present with all life brings you 24/7? Be sure to implement your new thought process and listening practice throughout the next week and take note of how your life changes as a result. Pay particular attention to your feelings about Life and to your ever-increasing ability to discern resonance within.

14. Describe how you now relate to the premise that you and God are One. How is that so regarding what God means to you? How you and God engage life lovingly? How you and God lovingly create?

15. Identify ways in which you can move toward a compelling presence with the process of going within to your inner Authority for Truth rather than depending on outside authority. Keep a journal regarding this transition and refine the process in ways that bring only Truth instead of illusion to your way of being.

16. Give consideration to befriending someone with whom you can share this journey. You may even want to form a loosely-defined support group, with no purpose other than to share progress. No one else can be an expert for you, so the purpose of the support group is to pour increasing degrees of loving energy on all who participate. This actually speeds up the process of healing and supplanting the old wine with the new. Be careful not to be duped into seeking some unneeded advice from a ready-made expert in such settings, for the only expert(ise) for you is in your own heart, with your inner Authority. Only you can get there to obtain it. If anyone does anything but refer you within for your answers, turn away and go within of your own volition.

17. Take your Bible or some other holy book in hand and find some stories that seem to call you to them. Read them literally first and then look at them as metaphors, symbolically. See what spiritual meaning they have for you and feel where that touches you. Celebrate this new meaning for you and practice this process regularly. Do the same with seemingly unrelated incidents that happen in your life. In addition to the material meaning, the one found outside of you, ask what spiritual meaning a particular incident may have. Practice simply wondering about it and listening carefully for the loving response that comes from within. You could find a new friend within as a result, a Friend you can come to trust without fail, One who will never let you down or lead you astray.

End Notes

- Katie, Byron with Mitchell, Stephen. *Loving What Is; Four Questions That Can Change Your Life.* New York: Three Rivers Press, 2002 (The method used to query Bartimaeus represents the method engendered by Byron Katie.) (323 pp.).

- *The Holy Bible; Authorized King James Version.* Boston: The Christian Science Publishing Society.

- Myss, Caroline. *Sacred Contracts; Awakening Your Diving Potential.* New York: The Three Rivers Press, 2002.

978-0-595-39833-1
0-595-39833-2

Printed in the United States
57134LVS00007B/59